Legends of
Giants
Baseball

Legends of Giants Baseball

Mike Shannon

Illustrated by Chris Felix, Scott Hannig, and Donnie Pollard

Black Squirrel Books™

Kent, Ohio

Frontis: John McGraw passing the torch to Bruce Bochy

Library of Congress Catalog Number 2015036111

ISBN 978-1-60635-290-8

Manufactured in Korea

Library of Congress Cataloging-in-Publication Data

Names: Shannon, Mike, 1951- author.

Title: Legends of Giants baseball / Mike Shannon ; illustrated by Scott Hannig, Chris Felix, and Donnie Pollard.

Description: Kent, Ohio : The Kent State University Press, [2016]

Identifiers: LCCN 2015036111 | ISBN 9781606352908 (Hardcover : alk. paper) ∞

Subjects: LCSH: San Francisco Giants (Baseball team)--History. | New York Giants (Baseball team)--History. | Baseball players--Biography.

Classification: LCC GV875.S34 A3 2016 | DDC 796.357/640979461--dc23 LC record available at http://lccn.loc.gov/2015036111

20 19 18 17 16   5 4 3 2 1

Contents

Foreword

The Giants were a superstar-oriented team long before the term "superstar" was coined.

Their lineage of peerless performers has remained virtually unbroken since the day in the mid-1880s when manager Jim Mutrie, exulting over a stirring victory, unintentionally gave the team its famous name by loudly exclaiming, "Look at my big boys! Look at my giants!"

Look at them, indeed. From Christy Mathewson to Mel Ott to Carl Hubbell to Willie Mays to Willie McCovey to Juan Marichal to Jack Clark to Will Clark to Barry Bonds, the Giants have ennobled the game with individuals whose potential for prodigious feats kept generations of fans from leaving their seats for a hot dog or a beverage. Consider the "Forever Giants," as the team's current ownership has dubbed its signature players, as well as the surprising list of stalwarts who made cameo appearances (Tony Lazzeri? Duke Snider? Warren Spahn? Hack Wilson?), and it should come as no surprise that the Giants have had more performers enshrined in baseball's Hall of Fame than any other franchise.

A handful of other organizations have won more World Series. But for sheer entertainment value, it's tough to beat what unfolded from Coogan's Bluff to Candlestick, as well as AT&T Park and a few other great ballyards.

The memorable Giants weren't simply elite performers. They were originals.

There were pitchers, and then there was Mathewson, the "Big Six" who became a national hero. Or Hubbell, with his confounding screwball. Or Marichal, with his impossibly high leg kick that described an exclamation point, which, figuratively speaking, punctuated his mastery of a vast assortment of deliveries.

There were infielders, and then there was Frankie Frisch, the "Fordham Flash" who played second and third base with equal proficiency in his early Major League career.

There were sluggers, and then there was Ott, who triggered his powerful swing with a kids-don't-try-this-at-home hoist of his right foot. Nowadays, he'd have

batting coaches who teach cookie-cutter swings scurrying for their DVDs of proper hitting fundamentals.

There were ballplayers, and then there was Mays. Enough said.

Needless to say, this is a ball club that boasts an enduring history. For instance, Hall of Fame first baseman Roger Connor, a member of the inaugural 1883 team who's lionized in these pages, still ranks among the franchise's all-time Top Ten in several major offensive categories.

This history continues to write and rewrite itself. Buster Posey, who has prompted comparisons to the sport's greatest catchers during his relatively brief career, hit a grand slam and stole a base in a June 2015 contest at Los Angeles. This made him the first Giants catcher to record both feats in the same game since Roger Bresnahan did it in 1903. (Posey's reaction: "It's cool.")

As welcome as Posey's appreciation was, many fans and readers might feel compelled to seek a deeper, broader perspective on the great men and great events in Giants history. To have this perspective delivered in All-Star fashion, here's where Posey, Bresnahan, Ott, and even Mays must cede the batter's box to Mike Shannon, who authors baseball books like Marichal formerly produced 20-win seasons—with regularity and excellence.

Mike's baseball pedigree is flawless. He has resided for decades in and around Cincinnati, steeping him in the flavor of the game that's unique to the birthplace of the big leagues. As the founder of the Casey Award, given to the author of each year's best baseball book, he knows the art of reviving the game's oldest tales and conveying its contemporary charm.

Moreover, growing up as a Mays acolyte, Mike learned to recognize a good ballplayer when he saw one. Reading this compendium of Giants legends will awaken the glories of the distant past and sweeten cherished memories of the club's recent World Series triumphs. Don't leave your seat.

Chris Haft

*Giants Beat Reporter
for MLB.com*

Introduction

Life is a mystery. Not just in general but in the particular as well. Many people live their entire lives as strangers—to themselves. The biggest riddle in my own life centers around how a kid growing up in Jacksonville, Florida—a professional baseball backwater in the early 1960s—became a passionate fan of a team a continent away from the sunbaked, palm tree–lined sandlots of north Florida. The short answer is Willie Mays (a great answer to any question), whom I idolized from a very early age. Exactly what drew me like a magnet to anything Mays, such as baseball cards, magazine covers, and Mays-endorsed baseball equipment, is hard to say; but because Willie was a Giant, the San Francisco Giants became de rigueur my favorite team.

Loving the Giants in my old neighborhood was nothing like being invested in the baseball turf wars of New York City in the fifties. Looking back now, it seems that most of the kids in my corner of that halcyon world were front-runners (which means they professed to be Yankees fans most of the time) or fans of the teams of their fathers, many of whom had migrated from colder parts of the country. I got into my share of fights as a boy but never received a bloody nose defending the honor of my favorite major league baseball team. On the other hand, it wasn't always easy being a San Francisco Giants fan.

A gangly Little League pitcher for the San Souci Saints, with an absurdly high leg kick fashioned after Juan Marichal's, I thrilled to the Giants' capturing of the NL flag in the summer of 1962. The seven-game loss to the Yankees in the World Series was a letdown, of course, but, like Giants' fans everywhere, I knew that with names like Cepeda, Perry, McCovey, Hart, Bolin, Davenport, and Alou (in addition to Mays and Marichal) in the fold, the future was bright and certain of World Championships. The Dodgers won in 1963 and the Cardinals in '64, and then for five straight years—from my last year in Catholic grade school at Assumption through my senior year at Bishop Kenny High School, years when I began to understand baseball and what it takes to win in the big leagues—the Giants finished in second place, every single year. Though

unbidden, this run of futility presented useful lessons, about hope and loyalty, stoicism and persistence.

Through college and marriage, the formation of a large and wonderful family and a career devoted to baseball literature, I remained a Giants fan. The disasters of the 1989 and 2002 World Series reinforced the lessons of my Giants youth, while deepening the accompanying frustration. And then out of nowhere came 2010! A seemingly miraculous gift I almost didn't believe. And when 2012 and 2014 followed, the satisfaction and sense of relief turned into incredulous joy that bordered on delirium.

The players didn't stop to muse about what their triumphs meant to fans like me, old men who'd gotten used to disappointment rooting for the Giants before the players had even been born. But such awareness will eventually come to them, at least to those contemplative, empathetic, and humble enough to realize how fortunate they have been to wear the uniform and help provide some happiness to the millions, about whom Milton might have been speaking when he wrote: "They also serve who only stand and wait"—"and cheer," I'll add. In 2013 I found a book in a secondhand store in my old hometown of Jacksonville about the 1951 National League pennant race and one such Giants' player, who'd inscribed it: "To Cliff and Betty—A couple of swingers to be sure from a guy who had one good swing in his life. With always my best wishes, Bobby Thomson."

This book, then, is a thank-you to Bobby and to Buster and MadBum, to Pablo and Pence, to Brian Wilson and Sergio and both Brandons, to all the guys on all three of those teams, to the Giants of my youth and yours, and to all the Giants stretching back to the days of John McGraw and Christy Mathewson and before that, to the very beginning, in 1883 when owner John B. Day's team was known simply as "the New Yorks." It's a book I loved every minute working on for six months, a book that has been a long time in the making.

What makes this Giants book special and different from every other volume on the team is the spectacular artwork by Chris Felix, Scott Hannig, and Donnie Pollard. These dear friends poured their hearts, as well as their enormous talents, into the project, and I haven't the words to express my admiration and gratitude for their work, beyond declaring that I am proud to have supplied the text that accompanies their amazing portraits.

I also thank the professionals at Kent State University Press for their superb efforts in doing all the things necessary to make the book a reality: Director Will Underwood, Managing Editor Mary D. Young, and Marketing Manager Susan Cash. Finally, I tip my cap to Giants fans everywhere. No matter what else may divide us, our love of the greatest baseball team in history unites us.

MIKE SHANNON
May 2015, Cincinnati, Ohio
Ad majorem Dei gloriam

Legends of
Giants
Baseball

1883–1925

Roger Connor

In the beginning, players for New York's National League team were known as the Gothams. They received their far more famous and permanent nickname after manager Jim Mutrie marveled one day at the size of his players: "Ah my big fellows . . . my giants." The biggest and strongest of Mutrie's Giants was Roger Connor, a power-hitting Hercules with a handlebar mustache and an imperious bearing who ended his eighteen-year major league career as the all-time home-run and triples champion of the nineteenth century. Giants' fans loved him and affectionately referred to him as "Dear Old Roger."

Connor was born July 1, 1857, in Waterbury, Connecticut, the city he embraced as home his entire life. After shaky trials with several minor league outfits, including one in Waterbury, Connor had success playing for a team in Holyoke, Massachusetts (National Association), in 1879. Roger's hitting impressed Bob Ferguson, manager of an opposing NA team, who signed the youngster after he was hired to lead the newly formed National League team in Troy, New York.

Even with other Hall of Fame talent such as Tim Keefe, Mickey Welch, and Buck Ewing on board, the Trojans were not very good. In 1880, his rookie year, neither was Connor as a left-handed–throwing third baseman. He was switched to first base the next year and played that position the rest of his career, excepting brief stints in center and at second base. Connor was not the most graceful of fielders, but he made a big target and became adept at digging out throws in the dirt. He eventually led the league in fielding percentage four times.

Hitting was never his problem. He hit .332, .292, and .330 in his three seasons with Troy and in 1882 led the league in triples, with 18. When the Trojans disbanded after the '82 season, John B. Day bought the players' contracts and assigned most of the players, including

Connor, to his New York National League team. For most of the next decade (1883–91, 1893) Connor was a terror in the heart of the Giants' batting order. During his first season with the Giants, he batted .357, and in 1886 he hit such a tremendous home run that the fans took up a collection to buy him a $500 gold watch. He hit over .300 six times for the Giants and 11 times overall. He won the NL batting crown in 1885 (.371) and led the league in triples (20) in 1886 and RBI (130) in 1889.

Ironically, the only year Connor led a league in home runs was 1890, when he swatted 14 for the New York club in the Players League, the short-lived (one year) circuit the players formed and ran in response to ill treatment by the owners of National League teams. Nevertheless, 1890 was a record fourth year in a row that Roger homered in double figures. His career total of 138 ranked first until 1921, when Babe Ruth surpassed it.

Connor was surprisingly fast for such a big man. He was a ferocious base runner and mastered what today is called the pop-up slide. Although the records are incomplete, he stole at least 244 bases, and his speed undoubtedly contributed to his total of 233 triples, the fifth-best mark in history. For years reference books listed Connor as a left-handed hitter, but recent research indicates that he switch-hit at least occasionally and that he definitely was the first switch-hitter to homer from both sides of the plate in one game.

Connor had good years for both Philadelphia and the St. Louis Browns after the Giants twice mistakenly believed him to be finished. He loved the game so much he continued playing in the minors until he was 46 years old, in 1903. A devout Catholic and dedicated family man, Connor later worked as a school maintenance inspector in Waterbury and enjoyed modest success as a local real estate investor. He died in 1931 and was belatedly called to Cooperstown in 1976.

YEAR	TM	G	AB	R	H	HR	RBI	SB	BB	SO	AVG
1880–82	TRO (3 yrs)	249	1056	173	335	9	120	0	41	61	.317
1883–89, '91, '93–94	NYG (10 yrs)	1120	4346	946	1388	76	786	161	578	276	.319
1890	NYP (1 yr)	123	484	133	169	14	103	22	88	32	.349
1892	PHI (1 yr)	155	564	123	166	12	73	22	116	39	.294
1894–97	SLB (4 yrs)	351	1347	245	409	27	241	39	179	41	.304
Total (18 yrs)		1998	7797	1620	2467	138	1323	244	1002	449	.316

Buck Ewing

William "Buck" Ewing escaped the dirty streets of the hog-butchering capital of the world (Cincinnati) to become an original New York Giant, an innovative catcher without peer, and in the eyes of his contemporaries the greatest all-around baseball player of the nineteenth century. He was also the slyest of umpire baiters and a magnet for controversy.

Ewing was born on October 17, 1859, near Hillsboro, Ohio, but grew up in "Porkopolis," where, after leaving school, he drove a delivery wagon for a distillery. He made a name for himself playing weekend semipro ball and was recommended to the Reds, but they didn't recognize his talent. In 1880 he was signed by Rochester (New York) of the National Association and played there that summer, until the league folded. The team from Troy brought him to the big leagues at the end of the season and was so impressed with his catching that it signed him for 1881, despite his having batted .178 in his 13-game trial. When the Trojans disbanded two years later, Ewing signed with the Cincinnati Reds for the 1883 season but reneged on the deal in order to get a fatter contract from the newly formed National League Gothams (soon to be "Giants"), the first of several Ewing imbroglios.

The 5'10", 188-pound Ewing did most of his catching bare-handed or nearly so from the 45' and 50' distances in an era when only the most primitive protective equipment was available. To avoid injury and prolong his career, he played other positions from the start. He caught fewer than half (636) the games he played (1,315) and is one of the few players in ML history to play the outfield and every infield spot and catch at least 25 games.

When Ewing did catch, there was none better or more inventive. He became the first to move up right behind home plate and set up in a crouch, the first to make snap throws from a crouch, and the first to use something akin to the padded, pillow-shaped mitts of modern baseball. He had a bag full of infamous tricks (such as intentionally dropping the ball to deke a runner into an ill-advised steal attempt), he was a master at manipulating umpires by flattering them or inciting the crowd against them, and he had the most feared arm in the game.

Although Buck was a spray hitter who didn't believe in swinging from the heels, he was capable of prodigious blasts and became the first major leaguer to reach double figures in home runs, when he hit 10 in 1883. He batted .303 that year and hit over .300 nine more times, his high of .344 coming in 1893 with Cleveland when he also achieved highs in games (116), AB (500), runs (117), hits (172), and RBI (122). In his nine-year Giants career, Ewing batted .306—three points above his lifetime average.

Ewing had average speed but was a brilliant base runner and thief nonetheless; he was the only catcher to swipe four bases in one game. He also once stole his way around the bases, preannouncing the theft of home, to win an extra-inning game, a feat that inspired a popular lithograph, *Ewing's Famous Steal*.

Although he served as captain of the Giants' pennant-winning teams in 1888 and '89, Ewing ran afoul of some teammates, who thought he sometimes faked injuries to avoid catching, especially when the fire-balling Amos Rusie was pitching. As player-manager Ewing had a terrific year in 1890 for the New York Players League entry, but his reputation took another hit when the players suspected he'd been tempted, by cash considerations, to abandon them and return midseason to the National League.

After finishing as an outfielder with the Cleveland Spiders (NL) and a first baseman with Cincinnati, Ewing managed his hometown Reds for five seasons, successfully, and the Giants, unsuccessfully, for 62 games in 1900. He died of diabetes in Cincinnati six years later, at age 47. He was remembered years later by sportswriter Francis Richter as a perfect player: "a player without a weakness of any kind, physical, mental, or temperamental."

YEAR	TM	G	AB	R	H	HR	RBI	SB	BB	SO	AVG
1880–82	TRO (3 yrs)	154	645	108	165	2	59	0	18	26	.256
1883–89, '91–92	NYG (9 yrs)	734	2957	643	905	47	459	178	211	194	.306
1890	NYP (1 yr)	83	352	98	119	8	72	36	39	12	.338
1893–94	CLE (2 yrs)	169	711	149	225	8	161	65	65	27	.317
1895–97	CIN (3 yrs)	175	698	131	211	6	132	75	59	35	.303
Total (18 yrs)		1315	5363	1129	1625	71	883	354	392	294	.303

John Montgomery Ward

A star on the mound and in the field, Montgomery "Monte" Ward was more than an outstanding baseball player. This natural leader, who became the player-manager of the New York Giants and two other major league teams, founded and became president of the Base Ball Player's Brotherhood, the organization that rebelled against the establishment to form its own league. As such, after Marvin Miller, Ward is the most important union figure in baseball history.

Montgomery Ward ("John" was a nickname) was born March 3, 1860, into a middle-class family in Bellefonte, Pennsylvania, and orphaned by the time he was a young teenager. A guardian angel helped him attend Penn State University, but he was kicked out after one year. He bounced from one insolvent minor league outfit to another and then halfway through the 1878 season caught on with Providence of the National League.

Firing fastballs and curves from a slight corkscrew windup, Ward was an immediate sensation. He went 22–13 with a league-best ERA of 1.51 in '78 and the following year turned in a phenomenal performance, leading the league in wins (47), winning percentage (.712), and strikeouts (239). Ward had another big year in 1880 (39–24; 1.74 ERA) but had trouble adjusting after the pitching distance increased from 45 to 50 feet in 1881; after that, he began to play more and more games in the outfield. His arm also simply began to wear out. In 1879 and '80 he pitched 58 and 59 complete games, and he averaged 43 CG during his five-year run with Providence.

Ward signed with New York in 1883 as a pitcher, but he hurt his shoulder in 1884, and after recording a 3–3 record he never pitched again. He climbed off the mound with a 164–103 career record and a .614 winning percentage.

After playing the outfield and second base his first two years in New York, Monte became the Giants' regular shortstop and for five years (1885–89) excelled at the position, from which he commanded the team like a general. He hit over .300 three times—his high of .338 coming in 1887—and totaled more than 2,100 hits during his 17-year career. He was a superb base runner and set a franchise record of 111 steals in 1887.

In New York, Ward completed his education at Columbia University, where he went on to obtain a law degree. Immensely popular with the Giants' fans, the handsome and sophisticated Ward exuded class. He lived in the chic Metropolitan Hotel, far away from the Polo Grounds; hobnobbed with the wealthy; and married actress Helen Dauvray. He wrote penetrating articles on the business of baseball and in 1888 became the first player to author and publish a book without a ghostwriter. It's no wonder other players, teammates and opponents alike, regarded him highly.

After sparking the Giants to their second consecutive pennant, Ward went on Albert Goodwill Spalding's proselytizing baseball world tour in the winter of 1889 and returned to discover that NL owners were in the process of imposing a classification scheme and salary caps. He helped his outraged colleagues form a rebel circuit, the Players League; took control of the Brooklyn franchise as its player-manager; and led the Wonders to a second-place finish. Although the majority of the better players from both the NL and the American Association defected, the PL, unable to withstand the NL's machinations, folded after one season. The Brotherhood served a purpose nevertheless, tempering the worst of the owners' abuses.

Ward returned to the NL but stayed back in Brooklyn as the Bridegrooms' player-manager for the 1891 and '92 seasons and then retired after two final seasons back with the Giants. Thereafter, he had a successful law practice and lived comfortably on Long Island. He caught pneumonia on a hunting trip and died in Augusta, Georgia, in 1925. The National Baseball Hall of Fame immortalized him in 1964.

YEAR	TM	G	AB	R	H	HR	RBI	SB	BB	SO	AVG
1878–82	PRO (5 yrs)	374	1570	252	386	4	175	0	33	75	.246
1883–89, '93–94	NYG (9 yrs)	1072	4470	830	1248	17	548	332	219	200	.279
1890	BRP (1 yr)	128	561	134	188	4	60	63	51	22	.335
1891–92	BRK (2 yrs)	253	1055	194	285	1	86	145	118	29	.270
Total (17 yrs)		1827	7656	1410	2107	26	869	540	421	326	.275

Tim Keefe

He was a pioneer of the game who played in three different major leagues and pitched from three different distances. He led the NY Giants to their first two National League pennants. He was the second major leaguer to win 300 games and the first to throw and master the change-of-pace. And during a time when baseball had more than its share of roughnecks and dissolutes, he was a perfect gentleman and a stylish dresser. He was Timothy John Keefe, aka "Sir Timothy."

The son of a factory builder who spent three years of the Civil War in a Confederate prison making bullets because he refused to fight against his northern brethren, Keefe was born on January 1, 1857, in Cambridge, Massachusetts. Although his father wanted him to further his high school education or pursue a profession, Keefe was smitten by "base ball" and took menial jobs with a succession of businesses in order to play for their company teams. He turned pro in 1879, pitching for Utica, New Bedford, and Albany of the minor league National Association. The National League's Troy Trojans picked him up in time for him to start 12 games in 1880. His ERA of 0.86, the lowest qualifying mark ever, belied his mediocre 6–6 record.

The Trojans were not a winning ball club, and Keefe's record the next two years reflected that (18–27 and 17–26, despite ERAs of 3.24 and 2.49). When Troy disbanded after the 1882 season, magnate John B. Day purchased the contracts of the players. Day assigned most of the better Troy players to his newly formed New York Gotham outfit in the National League but Keefe to his club in the American Association, the Metropolitans. Keefe dominated the league, going 41–27, while leading the league in starts (68), complete games (68), IP (619), and strikeouts (359). He also won both ends of a doubleheader, allowing a total of three hits in the two games. After Keefe led the Mets to the AA pennant in 1884 with a 37–17 record, Day transferred him to his National League team, soon renamed the Giants.

Keefe was the best pitcher in the game the next four years (1885–88), posting records of 32–13, 42–20, 35–19, and 35–12. The 5'10" right-hander, who threw mostly side-armed, had a sizzling fastball that made his innovative pitch, the changeup, all the more effective. Tim was also not afraid to pitch inside, although he missed several weeks of the 1887 season, agonizing over having almost killed a batter with a beanball.

During this stretch, Keefe teamed with his old Troy mate, the diminutive Mickey Welch, another eventual 300-game winner, to form a two-man rotation that led the Giants to the first two pennants in franchise history, in 1888 and 1889. Keefe won 19 consecutive games in 1888 and then beat the AA-champion St. Louis club four times in a World Series–like postseason matchup. Keefe had to hold out to get it, but his contract for $4,500 made him the highest-paid player on the team.

In 1890 Keefe jumped to the Player's League New York team, also called the Giants, and went 17–11 before a broken finger ended his season. On June 4 he beat the Boston Reds 9–4 to notch his 300th major league victory. The ill-fated rebel circuit fell apart after its one season, and Keefe returned to the real Giants. Ineffective, he was released in July '91 and signed with the Phillies, with whom he finished his career. He coached college baseball, sold real estate in his native Cambridge, and died in 1933.

Although Keefe pitched his entire career except his final season from the 50-foot distance, no one doubted he would have been just as dominant from 60'6". He was elected to the Hall of Fame in 1964.

YEAR	TM	W	L	ERA	GS	CG	SHO	IP	H	R	BB	SO
1880–82	TRO (3 yrs)	41	59	2.64	99	98	5	884	869	489	177	253
1883–84	NYA (2 yrs)	78	44	2.34	126	124	9	1102	868	440	179	693
1885–89, '91	NYG (6 yrs)	174	82	2.53	269	252	22	2265	1913	1077	580	1303
1890	NYP (1 yr)	17	11	3.38	30	23	1	229	225	137	89	89
1891–93	PHI (3 yrs)	32	29	3.21	70	57	2	569.2	563	328	208	226
Total (15 yrs)		342	225	2.63	594	554	39	5049.2	4438	2471	1233	2564

Christy Mathewson

Christy Mathewson was hands down the best pitcher to ever wear a Giants uniform. In fact, the tall, handsome, college-educated gentleman who dominated baseball's golden age remains one of the greatest hurlers the game has produced, in any era. He became America's first universally admired sports hero, and his early death at age 47 deeply saddened the baseball world.

Born August 12, 1880, in Factoryville, Pennsylvania, Mathewson exhibited a gifted right arm as a young teenager pitching for the men's town team. He honed his talent pitching for Bucknell University and impelled the lowly Giants to purchase his contract on the basis of his 20–2 record for Norfolk in 1900. After the Giants returned him to Norfolk because he lost his first three decisions, the Cincinnati Reds picked him up for $100. Coming to their senses, the Giants reacquired Mathewson in exchange for washed-up pitcher Amos Rusie, in the worst trade the Reds ever made.

"Matty" went 20–17 for the Giants in 1901 but fell to 14–17 the next year, despite an ERA of 2.06. Halfway through that 1902 season, John McGraw took over as Giants manager. He put an immediate stop to his predecessor's experimental use of Mathewson as a position player, and the fortunes of Mathewson and the Giants skyrocketed. "Big Six," as Mathewson was dubbed, after New York's fastest fire engine, won 30 or more games and led the league in strikeouts each of the next three years. The Giants won the pennant in 1905 and then rode Matty's arm to victory in the World Series. Mathewson shut out the Philadelphia A's three times, surrendering a total of 14 hits. Little wonder that A's manager Connie Mack later praised him as "the greatest pitcher who ever lived. He had knowledge, judgment, perfect control, and form. It was wonderful to watch him pitch when he wasn't pitching against you."

At a time when ballplayers were considered uncouth rowdies, the aristocratic Mathewson stood out like an orchid among the weeds. He made a stark contrast to the pugnacious, foul-mouthed McGraw, yet the two became lifelong best friends, and McGraw even regarded the pitcher as his adopted son. A trick pitch added to Mathewson's allure: his famous "fadeaway," which today is known as a screwball, a breaking ball that moves opposite of the normal direction. Mathewson didn't throw the fadeaway often, but its threat made him that much harder to hit.

Mathewson was the quintessential workhorse, piling up 300+ IP 11 times and pitching an amazing 434 complete games. A model of efficiency as well, he often needed no more than 75 or 80 pitches to vanquish an opponent, and he issued walks very sparingly; in 1913 he pitched 68 consecutive innings without allowing a free pass. He was the unquestioned ace of the Giants' staff for a decade and a half, winning the team's pitching Triple Crown seven times.

Matty won 20 or more games 13 times, with a high of 37 wins in 1908. He led the National League in wins four times, strikeouts five times, shutouts four times, and ERA five times. Five times he fashioned ERAs under 2.00, with his three lowest coming in at 1.14, 1.28, and 1.43. His lifetime ERA of 2.13 is fifth best of all time. He finished his career third all-time in shutouts and tied for third in wins. Even for the dead ball era, these numbers are scintillating.

The Giants won three more pennants behind Mathewson but no more World Series. In 1916 Matty was dealt to Cincinnati so he could begin a managerial career. In 1918, against the wishes of his wife, Jane, he enlisted in the United States Army as a captain and served in Europe in the Chemical Warfare Service. During training he was accidentally gassed, and exposure to the poison may have left him more susceptible to the disease (tuberculosis) that caused his death in 1925. A member of the first class elected to the Hall of Fame in 1936, along with Ty Cobb, Babe Ruth, Honus Wagner, and Walter Johnson, Christy Mathewson is remembered today as a true legend of the game.

YEAR	TM	W	L	ERA	GS	CG	SHO	IP	H	R	BB	SO
1900–16	NYG (17 yrs)	372	188	2.12	551	434	79	4779.2	4204	1613	847	2504
1916	CIN (1 yr)	1	0	8	1	1	0	9	15	8	1	3
Total (17 yrs)		373	188	2.13	552	435	79	4788.2	4219	1621	848	2507

Amos Rusie

Amos Wilson Rusie was not nicknamed "The Hoosier Thunderbolt" just because he was a pitcher from Indianapolis, Indiana. Oh no. People called him that because he may have been the fastest pitcher of all time. Connie Mack and John McGraw certainly thought so. And one Cubs player who'd seen the Rusie fastball up close said, "He drove the ball at you with the force of a cannon. It was like a white streak tearing past you." Rusie's heater was so fast and so dangerous, in fact, that it brought about the most significant rules change in the game's history: the increase of the distance between home plate and the pitching rubber from 50 feet to the current 60'6".

Born May 30, 1871, in Mooresville, Indiana, Rusie grew up in Indianapolis and played semipro ball as an outfielder. He came on in relief one day, and it was immediately obvious that he was born not to hit baseballs but to throw them. After Amos shut out the National League's Boston and Washington teams in exhibition games as an 18-year-old for an amateur outfit called the Sturm Avenue Never Sweats, the League's Indianapolis contingent signed him in 1889. When the Indianapolis team folded after the '89 season, the NL assigned six of the Hoosier team's players, including Rusie, to the New York Giants, who were suffering significant defections to the upstart Players League.

In his first season with the decimated Giants, the right-handed Rusie lost more games (34) than he won (29), but he lowered his ERA (2.56) by more than two-and-a-half points from his rookie year and thrilled fans around the league with his powerful arm. At 6'1" and 200 pounds, Rusie was a big man for his day, and the same size and strength that enabled him to throw so hard that his catcher kept a sheet of iron in his mitt also caused his weakness: a lack of control. In 1890 he led the NL in both strikeouts (341) and walks (289), setting a pattern that prevailed throughout his career. He led

the league in walks the next four years, each year totaling more than 200 free passes. To this day, Rusie owns four of the Top Ten highest season bases on balls totals, and he ranks seventh all-time in walks, despite pitching only nine full years. On the positive side, he led the NL in strikeouts four of the next five years (1891–95).

When the Giants' defectors returned in 1891, Rusie began winning. He posted the first of four consecutive 30+ win seasons (two before the rubber was moved back and two after, beginning in 1893); and on July 31 he became the youngest pitcher ever (at 20 years and two months) to throw a no-hitter, beating Brooklyn 6–0. His best year came in 1894, when he won the NL Triple Crown (36–13/2.78/195).

Rusie was as tough a negotiator as he was a pitcher and had several salary disputes with the Giants. The worst came after the penurious Andrew Freedman bought the club in 1895. Freedman, who alienated everyone, fined Rusie many times during that season on trumped-up charges, deducted the money from his final paycheck, and tried to foist on him an unfair contract for the coming year. Rusie retaliated by holding out all of 1896 and by suing Freedman. Afraid the suit might endanger the reserve clause and unhappy at the loss of Rusie as a drawing card, the other NL owners banded together to meet his monetary requirements themselves.

Rusie led the NL in ERA (2.54) again in 1897 and won 20 games the following year before hurting his arm on a pickoff throw to first base. He tried to rehabilitate the arm by sitting out two years, but he was out of gas. He helped the Giants one more time, going to the Cincinnati Reds in a trade for a winless Christy Mathewson. After working as the superintendent of the Polo Grounds and at a number of other jobs, Rusie retired in Seattle, where he died in 1942 in a car crash. He was elected to the Hall of Fame in 1977.

YEAR	TM	W	L	ERA	GS	CG	SHO	IP	H	R	BB	SO
1889	IND (1 yr)	12	10	5.32	22	19	1	225	246	181	116	109
1890–95, '97–98	NYG (8 yrs)	234	163	2.89	403	372	29	3531.2	3100	1862	1588	1835
1901	CIN (1 yr)	0	1	8.59	2	2	0	22	43	25	3	6
Total (10 yrs)		246	174	3.07	427	393	30	3778.2	3389	2068	1707	1950

Roger Bresnahan

One of the smartest major leaguers to ever wear "the tools of ignorance" was a resourceful Irishman with the gift of blarney named Roger Philip Bresnahan. Credited with the invention of baseball shin guards, Bresnahan became Christy Mathewson's favorite target and helped the New York Giants win their first pennant (1904) and first World Championship (1905) under the reign of maniacal manager John McGraw. No less an expert than Branch Rickey regarded Bresnahan as the greatest catcher of all time, and it was Bresnahan who in 1945 became the first twentieth-century backstop to be elected to the National Baseball Hall of Fame.

Bresnahan broke into the major leagues as a pitcher, and he became known as "The Duke of Tralee" after he told gullible sportswriters that he'd learned how to throw curveballs by flinging potatoes back in his native land. While Bresnahan's parents were from Tralee in County Kerry, Roger was born (June 11, 1879) in Toledo—in Lucas County, Ohio.

A catcher for Toledo Central High, Bresnahan was made into a pitcher by a summer league coach who wanted to take advantage of his strong arm. He pitched and caught after he turned pro with independent Lima, but when he was called up to Washington of the National League at the end of the 1897 as an 18-year-old, it was strictly as a pitcher. He was raw but successful, twirling a shutout in his first game and posting a 4–0 record. The next spring he balked at being sent down to start the season in the minors, so Washington released him. After extremely brief stints with Toledo, Minneapolis, and Chicago, he finally established himself as a major leaguer in 1901, appearing in 86 games, 69 of them as a catcher, for Baltimore of the new American League. Halfway through the next season, he jumped with his Irish pal John McGraw to the rebuilding New York Giants.

Although remembered as a catcher, Bresnahan was fast afoot and one of baseball's most versatile players ever. During his major league career, he swiped 212 bases and played games at every position on the field. In 1903, when the Giants climbed to second place in McGraw's first full season, and again in 1904, he was the Giants' regular center fielder and leadoff hitter. He had the best year of his career, statistically, in 1903, when he batted .350 (fourth in the league) with 55 RBI, 34 stolen bases, and an on-base percentage of .443—all career highs. Altogether, he posted an OBP of .400 or better eight times.

Bresnahan became the Giants' regular catcher in 1905, and it was immediately clear that he was cut out for the job. Obsessed, like McGraw, with winning, Roger was adept at the position's mental as well as physical requirements. Observers raved about the strength and accuracy of his arm, and Mathewson loved him, calling him "as brainy as he is tough." In the World Series that year, he was behind the plate, calling pitches for all four of the Giants' shutout victories over the Philadelphia A's: three by Mathewson and one by Joe McGinnity. Roger also batted leadoff all five games and led all hitters in average and on-base percentage.

In 1907, tired of the beating his legs were taking from wild pitches, slung bats, and sliding base runners, Bresnahan donned cricket shin guards; he was the first catcher to wear such protection outside the uniform. The practice was roundly ridiculed but caught on swiftly with other catchers. Bresnahan's seven-year Giants career ended after the 1908 campaign, when McGraw did Roger a favor by trading him to St. Louis so he could become the player-manager of the Cardinals. The woeful Cards improved to fifth in 1911, but Bresnahan was canned after his fourth year at the helm because of his impertinence toward owner Helene Britton. St. Louis sold him to the Cubs, with whom he ended his career. He later coached for McGraw and the Detroit Tigers.

YEAR	TM	G	AB	R	H	HR	RBI	SB	BB	SO	AVG
1897	WAS (1 yr)	6	16	1	6	0	3	0	1	0	.375
1900	CHC (1 yr)	2	2	0	0	0	0	0	0	0	.000
1901–02	BAL (2 yrs)	151	530	70	143	5	66	22	44	0	.270
1902–08	NYG (7 yrs)	751	2499	438	731	15	291	118	410	0	.293
1909–12	STL (4 yrs)	289	803	92	221	4	106	32	160	45	.275
1913–15	CHC (3 yrs)	247	631	81	151	2	64	40	99	54	.239
Total (17 yrs)		1446	4481	682	1252	26	530	212	714	99	.279

Iron Man McGinnity

As a young professional pitcher, Joseph Jerome McGinnity stumbled into a nickname when, in response to a reporter's question about his off-season occupation, he said, "I work in my father-in-law's foundry in Oklahoma. I'm an iron man." He earned that same nickname many times over after he became a tireless workhorse in the big leagues, singlehandedly pitching doubleheaders and setting labor and longevity records that still exist today.

Born on March 20, 1871, in Cornwall Township, Illinois, Joe McGinnity became a coal miner at a very young age, after his father was killed in a mining accident. He first gained notoriety while pitching for semipro teams in the coal-mining town of Krebs, Oklahoma. After pitching himself out of minor league baseball with lackluster seasons (1893, '94) at Montgomery of the Southern Association and Kansas City of the Western League, he turned to operating a saloon in Springfield, Illinois. A tough Irishman with a stocky build, McGinnity performed the saloon's bouncer duties himself. During this time, he returned to semipro ball and developed a baffling, slow-curving "upshoot" ball (or riser) that he launched with a submarine delivery. He got a second chance in pro ball with Peoria in 1898 and made the most of it, allowing fewer hits than IP and chalking up more strikeouts than walks for the first time in his career.

The next year, Joe made his National League debut as a 28-year-old rookie with John McGraw's Baltimore Orioles. Employing an average fastball, multiple arm slots, and his trick pitch, which he called "Old Sal," McGinnity went 28–16. He led the league in wins, ranked second in games (48), third in ERA (2.68), and fourth in IP (366.1). His nickname went into common use after he pitched in six games in one week in October, winning five of them.

McGinnity joined the Brooklyn Superbas in 1900 and led the club to the NL pennant and victory in the postseason *Chronicle-Telegraph* Cup series. He again won a league-leading 28 games, while cutting his losses to eight, and he also led the league in winning percentage (.778) and IP (343).

Brooklyn's failure to treat Joe fairly, financially, made it easy for him to decide to rejoin McGraw in Baltimore in 1901 for the American League's inaugural season. He won 26 and led the league in games, games started, complete games, and IP. He also pitched two doubleheaders, splitting them both.

When McGraw jumped back to the National League in July 1902 to manage the Giants, McGinnity went with him. For the next four years (1903–06) Joe and Christy Mathewson formed one of the best one-two pitching punches in history. McGinnity went 31–20, 35–8, 21–15, and 27–12 and posted ERAs of 2.43, 1.61, 2.87, and 2.25. He led the league in wins three times, in games five consecutive years (1903–07), and in IP twice. His 48 starts and 434 IP in 1903 remain major league records. McGinnity pitched three more doubleheaders, all in August 1903, and won all six games.

A sore loser and willing brawler, the Iron Man was hit with fines and suspensions on several occasions and was almost banned from the American League for spitting in an umpire's face. He was McGraw's kind of player, but after he turned in a .500 season (18–18) in 1908, Mac was ready to let him go. McGinnity won 151 games for the Giants in six-and-a-half years and left the team with the franchise's second-best ERA (2.38) and fourth-best winning percentage (.632). His 24.6 wins per season is a major league record.

McGinnity loved pitching so much he returned to the minors in 1909 and kept at it until 1925, when he won his final game—at age 54. He won 235 more games, giving him a composite total of 486 professional victories, second only to Cy Young. His greatness was recognized by his election to the Hall of Fame in 1946.

YEAR	TM	W	L	ERA	GS	CG	SHO	IP	H	R	BB	SO
1899	BAL (1 yr)	28	16	2.68	41	38	4	366.1	358	164	93	74
1900	BRK (1 yr)	28	8	2.94	37	32	1	343	350	179	113	93
1901–02	BAL (2 yrs)	39	30	3.52	66	58	1	580.2	631	319	142	114
1902–08	NYG (7 yrs)	151	88	2.38	237	186	26	2151.1	1937	774	464	787
Total (10 yrs)		246	142	2.66	381	314	32	3441.1	3276	1436	812	1068

Larry Doyle

It's one of the simplest but most meaningful lines ever uttered by a ballplayer: "Gee, it's great to be young and a Giant." So said "Laughing Larry" Doyle, who had plenty to be giddy about, as his talent on the diamond saved him from a life of drudgery and danger in the coal mines and made him a cornerstone of the John McGraw–led New York Giants teams that fashioned the best overall record during baseball's dead ball era.

Born July 31, 1886, in Caseyville, Illinois, Lawrence Joseph Doyle did, in fact, work underground for five years in the Breese, Illinois, coal mine about 40 miles east of St. Louis. Previously a weekend warrior who played for pass-the-hat money, Larry turned pro in 1906, joining the Class D Mattoon (Illinois) club in the nick of time, as a cave-in at the Breese mine on Christmas Eve killed six miners. Doyle made the jump to Class B Springfield the next year but spent only half the season in the Three-I League, because the Springfield owner, Dick Kinsella, convinced McGraw to buy Larry's contract for $4,500, at the time the highest sum ever paid for a minor leaguer.

Doyle missed the game on his first day in the big city, as he got lost trying to find the Polo Grounds. In his debut the next day on July 22, 1907, McGraw started him at second base even though he'd been a third baseman in the minors. Doyle made a mental error late in the game that let in an insurance run for the victorious opponents, but McGraw wasn't worried. He saw that Doyle could handle the bat and knew his defense would improve as he became more familiar with the position. Doyle quickly took over for 38-year-old Tommy Corcoran, batting .260 in 69 games.

Doyle heard from the boo birds and newspaper critics when he got off to a slow start the next year, but McGraw stood by him and felt vindicated when Larry got hot and finished the season batting .308, third in the league behind only Honus Wagner and Giants team-mate Mike Donlin. Doyle hit over .300 in three of the next four years too, finishing fourth (.302) in the 1909 batting race and fifth (.330) in 1912, when his great all-around season earned him the Chalmers Award (a new Chalmers automobile) as the best player in the National League. In 1915 Doyle won the NL batting title with an average of .320, his fifth and final .300 season.

With Doyle anchoring the infield, the Giants won three NL pennants in a row (1911–13), although they lost all three World Series. For more than a decade, Larry was not only a Giants stalwart but one of the NL's biggest stars and most productive hitters as well. Although his totals are not gaudy by today's standards, he hit the second-most home runs in the league twice and finished in the Top Five five times. He led the league in hits twice and doubles and triples once and racked up five Top Five slugging percentages and four Top Five Total Bases rankings.

Well liked for his sunny disposition, Doyle was also highly respected for his baseball acumen. He served as the Giants' team captain from 1908 until his trade to Chicago in 1916, and it became customary for him to take over the ball club on the numerous occasions McGraw got himself tossed from the game.

Doyle and his wife, Gertrude, accompanied McGraw and a number of other Giants and Chicago White Sox players on Charles Comiskey's famous world tour of 1913–14, which barnstormed across the United States before spreading the gospel of America's game to Asia, the Middle East, and Europe. Few of the sojourners won at the casino in Monte Carlo, but Doyle was seen leaving with "two hats full of francs."

After retiring, Doyle managed a couple of the Giants' minor league teams. He contracted tuberculosis in 1942 and was admitted to the sanatorium in Saranac Lake, New York. He made a full recovery and resided in Saranac Lake until his death on March 1, 1974.

YEAR	TM	G	AB	R	H	HR	RBI	SB	BB	SO	AVG
1907–16, '18–20	NYG (13 yrs)	1622	5995	906	1751	67	725	291	576	245	.292
1916–17	CHC (2 yrs)	144	514	54	136	7	68	7	49	29	.265
Total (14 yrs)		1766	6509	960	1887	74	793	298	625	274	.290

Rube Marquard

Of all the New York Giants' many dead ball–era stars, none flared so brilliantly and briefly as a tall, good-looking, left-handed pitcher named Richard William Marquard—a baseball prodigal son who made the most of his moment in the sun. Recovering from an almost debilitating start, Marquard won 75 games in three years, helped the Giants win three straight pennants, and set a record for consecutive wins that remains the target for pitchers today.

Born October 9, 1886, in Cleveland, Ohio, Marquard grew up obsessed with baseball. He served as a batboy for the Cleveland Naps and hung around the players constantly, absorbing everything he could about the game. Somebody thought he resembled Philadelphia A's pitcher Rube Waddell and hung the same nickname on him. In 1906, in defiance of his father, Fred, a city engineer, who was dead set against a baseball career, the 19-year-old Marquard made a quixotic five-day journey via freight trains to Iowa for a tryout but failed to catch on with the Waterloo team.

Undeterred, Marquard returned to Cleveland, went to work for an ice cream company, and pitched so well for the company team that the Naps attempted to sign him. After rejecting a lowball offer from that team, Rube signed with Canton, Ohio, and won 23 games for them in 1907. He won 28 games the next year for Indianapolis and set off a bidding war by pitching a perfect game in his final outing. McGraw won the war, shelling out the highest amount ever paid for a minor leaguer and saddling Rube with another moniker: the "$11,000 peach."

A rough outing in his Giants debut at the end of 1908 caused Marquard to lose his confidence. Two years later, his record stood at 9–18 and critics derisively referred to him as McGraw's "$11,000 lemon."

Fortunately, Wilbert Robinson became a Giants coach in 1911, and under his encouraging tutelage Marquard turned around his career. He posted the highest winning percentage in the National League (.774) with a record of 24–7 and led the league in strikeouts with 237. He led the league in wins the following season with 26 and chalked up 23 more in 1913, while his ERAs for the three years were 2.50, 2.57, and 2.50. With Rube and his roommate Christy Mathewson leading the way, the Giants swept into the World Series all three years but lost each time.

Marquard was at his best in 1912, when he won 19 consecutive games over the first three months of the season. During this amazing streak, he beat every team in the league at least twice, and he defeated Brooklyn three times and Philadelphia and Boston four times each. Under today's rules he would have been awarded a 20th victory for a stint he made in relief. In the Series that fall, Marquard pitched two complete-game victories over the Red Sox, allowing one earned run over 18 IP.

The spoils of victory were many for Marquard, whose winning streak vaulted him to fame. He began writing a newspaper column and endorsing products and even starred in a silent movie about himself. Most sensationally of all, he began singing and dancing with a beautiful vaudevillian starlet named Blossom Seeley, who divorced her husband to marry Rube. Best of all, Fred Marquard finally decided that he was proud of his baseball-crazy son.

As quickly as Marquard became a star, he returned to lemon status, posting a 12–22 record in 1914. He did pitch a no-hitter in 1915 before McGraw let him move on to Brooklyn. Reunited with his mentor Robinson, Brooklyn's manager, Marquard turned in two more good seasons, going 13–6 in 1916 and 19–12 in 1917. He won 17 games for Cincinnati in 1921 but fizzled out with four losing seasons in Boston.

After baseball, Marquard settled in Baltimore and eventually married a rich widow. Lawrence Ritter's book *The Glory of Their Times* renewed Rube's fame and paved the way for his induction into Cooperstown in 1971.

YEAR	TM	W	L	ERA	GS	CG	SHO	IP	H	R	BB	SO
1908–15	NYG (8 yrs)	103	76	2.85	188	99	16	1546	1420	633	430	897
1915–20	BRK (6 yrs)	56	48	2.58	115	61	9	950	864	352	207	444
1921	CIN (1 yr)	17	14	3.39	36	18	2	265.2	291	123	50	88
1922–25	BOS (4 yrs)	25	39	4.44	68	19	3	545	658	335	171	164
Total (18 yrs)		201	177	3.08	407	197	30	3306.2	3233	1443	858	1593

Ross Youngs

Like the New York Yankees, the New York Giants had a star player who was cruelly cut down in his prime. Ross Youngs never delivered a poignant farewell at home plate as did Lou Gehrig, nor was the disease that killed him named after him; but his loss was nevertheless a devastating blow to the manager, teammates, and fans who loved him. He played only nine full seasons in the big leagues, but this was long enough to establish his greatness; most prominently, he left behind the fourth-highest career batting average (.322) in team history.

Born April 10, 1897, in Shiner, Texas, Royce Middlebrook Youngs first made a name for himself as a short, fast, powerful halfback at West Texas Military Academy. He began playing minor league baseball as a switch-hitting infielder at age 16 and was signed by the Giants after batting .362 for Sherman of the Western League. New York manager John McGraw took a special interest in the youngster and handed him over to Rochester skipper Mickey Doolan for the 1917 season with the warning: "I'm giving you a kid who is going to be a great player. Play him in the outfield. If anything happens to him, it's your ass."

Youngs feasted on International League pitching, earning an end-of-the-season call-up of seven games in which he hit .346. Batting strictly from the left side, he became the Giants' regular right fielder in 1918 and hit .302 in his rookie season. The next year, Youngs led the National League in doubles with 31 and hit .311, which was third in the league behind Edd Roush and Rogers Hornsby. He went on to hit over .300 six more times. He hit .351 to finish second in the 1920 NL batting race to Hornsby; and the .356 mark he recorded in 1924, the highest batting average of his career, was good enough for third place among all NL batters. He also achieved Top Ten batting averages in 1921 and '23.

A slashing line-drive hitter, Youngs was no fence buster, but he found many a gap, and his 93 career triples place him eighth on the franchise all-time list. "Pep," as McGraw called him for his hustling style of play, stole home 10 times and once hit three triples in a single game. He had a rocket for an arm and led the league in outfield assists three times. He became a master at playing the caroms off the close right-field wall at the Polo Grounds. With Youngs in the middle of the lineup, the Giants won four consecutive pennants (1921–24) and two World Series (1921, 1922).

In 1925 Ross batted .264; his only poor season not a normal slump but a symptom of his illness. In the spring of '26 he was diagnosed with Bright's disease, a terminal kidney ailment. The Giants hired a nurse to travel with him, and Youngs bravely played in 95 games, turning in one final .300 season. He died at the age of 30 the following October.

McGraw, who reportedly had been grooming Youngs to become his successor, took the young man's death especially hard. He lavished him with praise, saying, "He was the greatest outfielder I ever saw. He could do everything that a baseball player should do and do it better than most players. As an outfielder, he had no superiors. And he was the easiest man I ever had to handle. In all his years with the Giants he never caused one moment's trouble for myself or the club. On top of that, a gamer player than Youngs never played ball."

In 1928 the Giants hung a bronze plaque that paid tribute to Youngs, "A brave untrammeled spirit of the diamond," on the right field wall of the Polo Grounds. Though not asked to pay for the plaque, Giants fans insisted on doing so. The Veterans Committee voted Youngs into the Baseball Hall of Fame in 1972.

YEAR	TM	G	AB	R	H	HR	RBI	SB	BB	SO	AVG
1917–26	NYG (10 yrs)	1211	4627	812	1491	42	592	153	550	390	.322

Frank Frisch

Sometimes the one you love the most, you hurt the worst—words behind many a country love song but also as good an explanation as there is for the premature end to Hall of Famer Frankie Frisch's career with the New York Giants.

In 1926, as the Giants played poorly for the second year in a row after having won four straight pennants, the scathing criticism by fiery manager John McGraw became worse than ever. McGraw directed his most vicious abuse toward one of his all-time favorite players, second baseman Frankie Frisch, simply because Frisch was captain of the team. When the beaten-down Frisch could take it no more and went AWOL for a few days, his fate was sealed. In December McGraw made a sensational trade with the St. Louis Cardinals, acquiring six-time batting champ Rogers Hornsby, another future Hall of Famer, for pitcher Jimmy Ring and Frisch.

The banishment of Frisch was sad and ironic because as a player he was exactly like his mentor, McGraw: aggressive, hard-nosed, and highly competitive. He had come to the Giants in June 1919 straight from Fordham University, where he'd excelled at four sports and made Walter Camp's honorary All-American football squad in 1918. The Fordham baseball coach was Art Devlin, a former third baseman for the Giants. Despite being estranged from McGraw, Devlin wanted his prize prospect to go to no one else. In recommending Frisch, Devlin said, "This is a real ball player, Mac. A major league ball player. Right now."

While Frisch got his feet wet, playing sparingly that first year, McGraw took the youngster under his wing. He corrected Frisch's cross-handed swing from the left side, turning him into a proper switch-hitter; and moving him off shortstop, his college position, he played him the first few years at both third and second. Frisch became a regular in 1921 and had a marvelous season, collecting 211 hits (for a .341 average) and 100 RBI. He also led the National League in stolen bases with 49, giving impetus to his nickname "The Fordham Flash."

An expert bunter and superb place hitter, Frisch batted over .300 each of his final six seasons in New York (1921–26), with a high of .348 in 1923, when he led the league in hits with 223. He led the Giants in stolen bases seven times, hits four times, and batting average three times. "The Flash" was also extremely hard to strike out. In 1923, when he hit a career-high 12 home runs, he whiffed 12 times. In all, the .316 lifetime hitter batted 9,112 times and struck out a mere 272 times. Frisch did not have the best hands, but once he settled at second base, he was a fantastic defender who used his chest as a backstop and made diving stops and running catches all over the field. He was also a prime-time performer for McGraw, batting a composite .363 in four World Series.

Not surprisingly, the trade with St. Louis did not work out—for the Giants. Hornsby was almost as acerbic as McGraw, and he lasted exactly one year in New York before being deported to the Boston Braves. Though not warmly welcomed at first, Frisch won over the Cardinals' fans by putting together another great year in 1927, playing sterling defense at second and knocking out 208 hits for an average of .337. He helped St. Louis win pennants in 1928, 1930, and 1931, and midway through the '33 campaign he was named player-manager of the team. That team full of wild men, known as "The Gas House Gang," went on to win the flag and defeat Detroit in one of the most infamous and hotly contested World Series on record.

Frisch later managed the Pirates and Cubs, did broadcasting in Boston and New York, and in retirement in Delaware lived the life of an educated gentleman. The greatest second baseman in Giants franchise history, he entered the Hall of Fame in 1947, the cap on his plaque bearing no team initials.

YEAR	TM	G	AB	R	H	HR	RBI	SB	BB	SO	AVG
1919–26	NYG (8 yrs)	1000	4053	701	1303	54	524	224	280	139	.322
1927–37	STL (11 yrs)	1311	5059	831	1577	51	720	195	448	133	.312
Total (19 yrs)		2311	9112	1532	2880	105	1244	419	728	272	.316

Travis Jackson

Dictatorial manager John McGraw did not keep his New York Giants competitive for three decades by being sentimental. No, he ruthlessly discarded and acquired roster pieces the way a Vegas cardsharp plays poker, sometimes to the bewilderment of the team's supporters. Giants' fans howled loudly when McGraw traded shortstop Dave "Beauty" Bancroft, a future Hall of Famer, but McGraw knew that he had a younger replacement who would make the fans forget about Bancroft. The kid from Waldo, Arkansas, would be the linchpin of the best infield McGraw ever assembled, as well as the greatest Giants shortstop of the modern era.

Born on November 11, 1903, Travis Calvin Jackson went from Ouachita Baptist College to Little Rock of the Southern League to the New York Giants by the time he was 18 years old. In 1923, a season in which he appeared in 96 games, he served as a backup to Heinie Groh at third base and to Bancroft at short. On August 4 at Redland Field in Cincinnati he knocked in eight runs on two singles, a double, and a home run, impressing McGraw and paving the way for Bancroft's departure that fall. The next year, as the regular shortstop, Jackson played 151 games and batted .302, with 11 home runs (second on the team) and 76 RBI (third).

Given Jackson's southern heritage, his nickname "Stonewall" was perhaps inevitable, yet it also aptly conveyed his defensive abilities. Jackson had sure hands, a great arm, a quick release, and superb range. He led the National League in assists four times, in total chances three times, and in double plays and fielding percentage twice each. Joe Cronin, himself a great shortstop, called Jackson "as good a shortstop as ever lived." According to Frank Graham's 1952 Putnam history of the New York Giants, prior to the Giants acquiring slick-fielding second sacker Hughie Critz in early 1930, Jackson

had worn himself out trying to play short and second base. And no better testament of Jackson's baseball savvy was possible than Rogers Hornsby's declaration: "In all the years I watched him, playing with him and against him, I never saw him make a mistake."

Jackson hit over .300 five more times—with a high of .339 in 1930, when he was a member of the best hitting infield in baseball history. Jackson's average combined with Bill Terry's .401, Critz's .265, and Freddie Lindstrom's .379 resulted in a composite average of .349. During a three-year period (1925–27), Jackson was part of an all–Hall of Fame infield that included himself, Lindstrom at third base, Frank Frisch or Hornsby at second, and Terry or George Kelly at first. Though slight of stature—just 5'10", 160 pounds—Jackson was a productive as well as steady hitter. Normally a six-hole hitter, he drove in more than 75 runs per season seven times, and at the time of his retirement his lifetime total of 135 home runs was the most ever hit by a shortstop. He was also an expert bunter.

Selected to *The Sporting News* Major League All-Star Team in 1927, '28, and '29, Jackson was bothered by chronic right knee pain from the beginning of his career. He injured his left knee in 1932 and that winter had surgery on both knees. After playing in only 105 games in 1932 and '33 combined, he bounced back in 1934 to make the NL All-Star team, knocking in a career-best 101 runs. He moved to third base for his final two big league seasons.

After hanging up his glove, he coached for the Giants and managed more than a dozen minor league teams. He later battled tuberculosis and died in Waldo in 1987, five years after being elected to the Hall of Fame. He is the franchise leader in putouts and assists by a shortstop, and as a hitter he ranks in the franchise Top Ten in seven categories: games, at bats, hits, doubles, triples, RBI, and total bases.

YEAR	TM	G	AB	R	H	HR	RBI	SB	BB	SO	AVG
1922–36	NYG (15 yrs)	1656	6086	833	1768	135	929	71	412	565	.291

Bill Terry

Being offered an audition by John McGraw made most bush leaguers weak in the knees and nearly speechless with gratitude and joy. Not so Bill Terry, a young pitcher and first baseman in Memphis, who had one question: "What's the pay?" At first insulted by such effrontery, McGraw later decided he liked Terry's confident sense of self-worth and brought him into the New York Giants fold. It was one of the smartest moves McGraw ever made, as Terry not only became the team's brightest star for a decade and the last batter to hit .400 in the National League, but also the old man's successor as team manager.

Terry was born October 30, 1898, in Atlanta, Georgia, and grew up fast. His parents separated when he was thirteen, so he quit school to support his mother. "When I was fifteen I was doing a man's work," he once said. "I was unloading freight cars, throwing sacks of flour into trucks." He got an early start in pro baseball too and had success—he pitched a Class D no-hitter in 1915—but tired of the traveling and low pay. By the time McGraw found him, Terry had a wife and child, a home, a good job working for Standard Oil, and no desire to leave Memphis, even for the major leagues, unless the Giants made it worth his while.

During the tryout at the Polo Grounds, McGraw could see that Terry had a bright future—as a hitter, not a pitcher. He sent the left-hander (batting and throwing) down for seasoning, to Toledo, where "Memphis Bill" hit .336 in 1922 and .377 in 1923. Foreshadowing his future role with the Giants, Terry even managed the Mud Hens for part of the latter season.

Terry batted .239 as a rookie in 1924 while platooning at first base with George "High Pockets" Kelly but hit .429 in that fall's World Series. He became the Giants' regular first sacker the following year when he hit .319 and would go on to bat over .300 ten consecutive seasons (1927–36).

Terry was a strong man and had decent power, hitting 20 or more home runs three times, with a high of 28 in 1932. But instead of swinging for the fences, he preferred hitting vicious liners and driving the ball into the spacious alleys of the horseshoe-shaped Polo Grounds. He hit 30+ doubles nine times and in his career hit almost as many triples (112) as homers (154). He led the league in triples (20) in 1931. A perfectionist, Terry also made himself into the best fielding first baseman in the National League. He led his colleagues in fielding percentage twice, double plays three times, putouts and assists five times, and total chances per game nine times.

In 1929 Bill racked up 226 hits, while batting .372, the first of six seasons in which he would total 200 or more hits. His finest season came the next year, when he scored 139 runs, drove in 129, cracked 23 homers, and topped the league in hits (254) and batting average, with a mark of .401, 98 points higher than the league average. He missed winning a second batting title the next year by three hundredths of a point.

Halfway through the 1932 season, an exhausted and ill McGraw called it quits after three decades of managing. Despite Terry's frequent salary battles and his off-putting personality, which had endeared him to no one, McGraw named Terry as his successor. Terry won two pennants (1933, 1936) as a player-manager and a third in 1937 after he'd hung up his spikes. After a sixth-place finish in 1941, he resigned with the franchise's second-best winning percentage (.555, minimum 1,000 games managed).

Terry was never a favorite of sportswriters either, and they took their sweet time before electing him to the Baseball Hall of Fame in 1954, despite his unquestioned merits. He ran a successful auto dealership in Jacksonville, Florida, for many years before his death in 1989.

YEAR	TM	G	AB	R	H	HR	RBI	SB	BB	SO	AVG
1923–36	NYG (14 yrs)	1721	6428	1120	2193	154	1078	56	537	449	.341

Fred Lindstrom

"Some are born great. Some achieve greatness. And some have greatness thrust upon them." So said the Bard. Shakespeare never witnessed a baseball game, but two of his three descriptions perfectly fit New York Giants third baseman Frederick Charles Lindstrom, who certainly packed his share of excellence and controversy into his prematurely ended 13-year career.

Born November 21, 1905, in Chicago, Fred Lindstrom grew up a White Sox fan, had an unsuccessful tryout with the Cubs, and as a 16-year-old student at Chicago's Loyola Academy signed with the New York Giants. He played two years with the Toledo Mud Hens alongside Bill Terry and was brought up to New York in 1924 as a backup to the declining Heinie Groh. That fall, with only 52 major league games under his belt, after a knee injury incapacitated Groh, Fred suddenly found himself in the national spotlight. When he stepped in as the leadoff batter of the World Series in Washington, Lindstrom, at 18 years, 10 months, and 13 days, became the youngest player to ever appear in the Fall Classic. He became both a hero and the goat of the Series.

He rapped 10 hits, including four in one game against the redoubtable Walter Johnson, to bat .333, and he played well in the field, even collecting seven assists in Game 2, a record that lasted 26 years. When the seesaw Series was decided dramatically in Game 7, Lindstrom was right in the middle of the action. In the bottom of the eighth, a routine grounder to third hit a pebble and caromed over his head to allow two runs to score, tying the game 3–3. Then in the 12th, another bad hop grounder got past Fred to let in the Senators' winning run.

The youngster bounced back from this disappointment to hit .287 in 104 games in 1925, and he then batted .300 or higher in seven of the next eight seasons. Called "the last of the great place hitters," Lindstrom was very tough to strike out, especially in the clutch. After he led the National League in hits with 231 while batting .358 to finish second in the League MVP Award voting for 1928, sportswriters began to sing his praises. "An outstanding individual of the game," gushed Ken Smith of the *New York Evening Graphic,* "another Hornsby, Wagner, Cobb, or Speaker, this kid, ace fielder, hitter, thinker and runner." Fred's reputation soared even higher after he batted .379 (again on 231 hits) in 1930.

Lindstrom was one of the few players gutsy enough to talk back to the acerbic, Napoleonic John McGraw; yet McGraw esteemed him highly, putting him ninth on his list of the 20 greatest players of all time. However, Fred felt betrayed when he was not named the manager's successor, as he thought McGraw had promised he would be. The job went to Lindstrom's good friend Bill Terry, who traded Fred to Pittsburgh after the 1932 season, at Fred's own request.

In 1933, Fred's batting average was the Pirates' second highest and ranked in the NL Top Ten for the third and final time. His last hurrah came in 1935, when he drove the Cubs to the pennant, batting .427 during a stretch of 21 consecutive wins in September, as he either scored or drove in the winning run seven times. At age 30, while playing outfield for Brooklyn in 1936, he collided with infielder Jimmy Jordan and decided to hang 'em up in disgust.

He later managed a couple of minor league ball clubs, coached the baseball team at Northwestern University for 13 years, and served as postmaster of Evanston, Illinois, until 1972. Possessor of the seventh-highest lifetime batting average (.318) in Giants history, he entered the Hall of Fame in 1976, having been a member of New York's all–Hall of Fame infield that included Terry, Travis Jackson, and Rogers Hornsby.

YEAR	TM	G	AB	R	H	HR	RBI	SB	BB	SO	AVG
1924–32	NYG (9 yrs)	1087	4242	705	1347	91	603	80	263	213	.318
1933–34	PIT (2 yrs)	235	921	129	278	9	104	2	56	43	.302
1935	CHC (1 yr)	90	342	49	94	3	62	1	10	13	.275
1936	BRK (1 yr)	26	106	12	28	0	10	1	5	7	.264
Total (13 yrs)		1438	5611	895	1747	103	779	84	334	276	.311

Johnny Mize

Even though slugging first baseman Johnny Mize played for three of baseball's most storied franchises, he is best remembered as a New York Giant. Nicknamed the "Big Cat" for his ability to dig low throws out of the dirt, his graceful swing, and the casual way he leaned back to avoid brushback pitches, Mize led the 1947 Giants to a National League team home-run record, as he became the first NL left-handed batter to hit 50 or more homers in a season. The only regret Giants fans ever had about him was that his career with the team lasted a mere five years.

John Robert Mize was born January 7, 1913, in Demorest, Georgia, a relative, according to Mize's 1953 bio-instructional *How to Hit,* of both Babe Ruth and Ty Cobb. As a lad, he spent countless hours perfecting his hand-eye coordination hitting with a broomstick a tennis ball he would throw against a barn. As a high school sophomore, he played on the varsity baseball team of Piedmont College. He broke into pro ball at the age of 17 in 1930, signing with Greensboro, then a St. Louis Cardinals' affiliate.

Despite Mize's consistently battering minor league pitching, it took the burly slugger six years to get to the big leagues, due in part to the Cardinals' stocked farm system and in part to a leg problem that necessitated surgery in 1935. Mize immediately established himself as a star—he batted .329 as a rookie in 1936—and as that rare type of batter who hits for both power and high average while seldom striking out. Johnny batted .364 in 1937 and then .349 to cop the 1939 NL batting crown, while he led the league in home runs in 1939 and '40 and in RBI in 1940 and '41. In his six years with St. Louis, he averaged .336.

Tired of being underpaid by Cardinals' general manag-

er Branch Rickey, Mize asked to be traded and was dealt to the Giants on December 11, 1941. Although the Polo Grounds was not an ideal park for him to hit in, Johnny adjusted well to it. In 1942 he drove in 100+ runs for the sixth year in a row and batted .305. He lost the next three prime years of his career to service in the United States Navy. After the war, he hit .337 in 1946, and then came his monster year with the Giants: a league-leading 138 RBI and those 51 homers, which tied him for the league lead with Ralph Kiner. He also tied Kiner for NL home-run honors with 40 in 1948.

A victim of newly hired manager Leo Durocher's housecleaning, Mize was sold to the Yankees for $40,000 during the 1949 season. He left the Giants at age 36 with a lifetime average of .320, having hit 157 home runs for the team while striking out 163 times.

The Yankees were delighted to obtain Mize, even past his prime, and they utilized him as an occasional starter and premier pinch hitter. Manager Casey Stengel called him "a slugger who hits like a leadoff man." Mize, in fact, led the American League in pinch-hits three years in a row (1951–53). He helped the Yankees win five pennants in a row (1949–53), and his three self-proclaimed biggest thrills all came in World Series play. After his two-run ninth-inning single helped win Game 3 of the 1949 Series, sportswriter Dan Parker penned this ditty:

"Your arm is gone; your legs likewise,
But not your eyes, Mize, not your eyes."

Mize was the hero of the 1952 Series and the winner of the Babe Ruth Award for batting .400 with six RBI and home runs in three consecutive games. A ten-time All-Star, Mize made the Hall of Fame in 1981. His hometown dedicated a statue of him during its centennial in 1989.

YEAR	TM	G	AB	R	H	HR	RBI	SB	BB	SO	AVG
1936–41	STL (6 yrs)	854	3121	546	1048	158	653	14	424	279	.336
1942, '46–49	NYG (5 yrs)	655	2452	473	733	157	505	13	340	163	.299
1949–53	NYY (5 yrs)	375	870	99	230	44	179	1	92	82	.264
Total (15 yrs)		1884	6443	1118	2011	359	1337	28	856	524	.312

Sal Maglie

He was a late bloomer whose delayed development was further impeded by World War II and a costly mistake that made him an outlaw of "organized baseball." Yet, his purgatory led to his salvation, so that when he finally got a bona fide chance with the New York Giants, he became one of the nastiest, most feared, and most successful pitchers of his day. Salvatore Antony Maglie was "The Barber," an intimidator whose brushback pitches gave close shaves to the chins of any batters who dared stand too close to the plate. For three years he was almost unbeatable, and his seven-year winning percentage of .693 remains the highest in Giants franchise history.

Born April 26, 1917, in Niagara Falls, New York, Maglie broke into pro baseball in 1938 with the Buffalo Bisons of the International League, but he was woefully unprepared for such stiff competition. He did much better for single-A Elmira in 1941, causing the Giants to draft him. He made more progress at Jersey City in '42, but then World War II interrupted it. After receiving a deferment for a chronic sinus problem, he went home and spent the next two years working at a defense-related job. Despite Maglie's mediocre performance with Jersey City in 1945, the manpower shortage induced the Giants to promote him and give him 84 innings of work over 13 games.

Worried that he did not fit into the Giants' long-term plans and seduced by the promise of big money, Maglie headed south the next spring to play for Puebla in the newly formed Mexican League, which was attempting to operate as a third major league. The "outlaw" league folded after two years but not before Puebla's manager, Dolf Luque, the former Giants pitching coach, transformed Maglie into a carbon copy of himself as a younger, intense competitor. With the fervor of a drill sergeant, Luque taught Maglie to sharpen his curve and to pitch inside aggressively, using fear of the beanball as a weapon.

Maglie rejoined the Giants in 1950 after threatened legal challenges caused baseball to lift the five-year ban imposed on the "jumpers." The 33-year-old with the withering glare and perpetual five o'clock shadow was one of the game's best pitchers over the next three years, posting records of 18–4, 23–6, and 18–8. Maglie's mark of .818 in 1950 is the second-best one-season winning percentage in Giants history, while his 23 wins in '51 topped the National League and led New York to the pennant. Maglie was especially tough on the Giants' hated rivals, the Brooklyn Dodgers, against whom he fashioned a lifetime record of 23–11, including an 11–3 ledger in Brooklyn's Ebbets Field, a notorious hitter's ballpark. In 1953 back problems led to Maglie's only losing season as a Giant, but he bounced back to help New York win another pennant in 1954 with a 14–6 record. Just as Sal's career appeared to fizzle out in Cleveland, the Dodgers shocked their fans by purchasing his contract for $100 in early 1956. It was the best C-note Brooklyn ever spent. Maglie went 13–5, with an ERA of 2.87, to help the Dodgers win the pennant, and he even pitched a no-hitter on September 25 against the Phillies for good measure. He turned in a complete-game victory over the New York Yankees in Game 1 of the '56 World Series, and he pitched well in Game 5 too but lost to Don Larsen, who twirled the only perfect game in Series history. Maglie thus started the two most famous games of the 1950s, as he had gone the first eight innings of the deciding playoff game in 1951 and was in the clubhouse drinking a beer when Bobby Thomson hit "The Shot Heard 'Round the World" to beat the Dodgers.

Maglie's stint in the Bronx made him one of the few players to play for the Giants, Dodgers, and Yankees. He later coached for the Red Sox and Seattle Pilots, passing on what Luque had taught him.

YEAR	TM	W	L	ERA	GS	CG	SHO	IP	H	R	BB	SO
1945, '50–55	NYG (7 yrs)	95	42	3.13	171	77	20	1297.2	1216	512	434	654
1955–56	CLE (2 yrs)	0	2	3.87	2	0	0	30.2	32	16	9	13
1956–57	BRK (2 yrs)	19	11	2.90	43	13	4	292.1	248	107	78	158
1957–58	NYY (2 yrs)	3	1	3.12	6	1	1	49.1	49	18	16	16
1958	STL (1 yr)	2	6	4.75	10	2	0	53	46	31	25	21
Total (10 yrs)		119	62	3.15	232	93	25	1723	1591	684	562	862

Bobby Thomson

Moments before New York Giants third baseman Bobby Thomson went to bat on October 3 in the bottom of the ninth inning of the third and final playoff game to decide the 1951 National League pennant, manager Leo Durocher implored him, "If you ever hit one, hit one now." Two pitches later Thomson did just that, lining a three-run walk-off home run into the Polo Grounds' left-field bleachers to defeat the rival Brooklyn Dodgers 5–4, cap an incredible comeback that erased a 13½-game Dodgers lead in six-and-a-half weeks, and vault the Giants into the World Series. Called "The Shot Heard 'Round the World," the home run sent Giants fans (and radio broadcaster Russ Hodges) into a frenzy and bestowed baseball immortality on Thomson. In the minds of many fans, it remains the single greatest moment in baseball history.

The son of a Glasgow cabinetmaker, Robert Brown Thomson was born October 25, 1923, in Scotland and immigrated to New York as an infant. The relative ease with which he advanced to the major leagues made it seem as if "The Staten Island Scotsman," as Thomson became known, was destined for baseball fame. Signing with the Giants the day after his high school graduation in 1942, Bobby played 34 games in the low minors and then enlisted in the Air Force late in the year. After World War II ended, the Giants took all their players to spring training in 1946, which gave the unheralded Thomson a chance to impress. He made the Giants' AAA farm club, the Jersey City Giants, and performed so well that he earned a call-up to New York—batting .315 in 18 games.

The speedy Thomson, a converted infielder, became the Giants' regular center fielder the next year. He batted .283 with 85 RBI in 138 games and contributed 29 home runs to the Giants' major league record-setting total of 221. If not for the performance of Jackie Robinson, the Dodgers stalwart who broke the color barrier, Thomson probably would have scooped up NL Rookie of the Year honors for 1947.

After suffering from the sophomore jinx in '48, Bobby rebounded in 1949 to become the offensive star of the team that was in the midst of a makeover by new manager Leo Durocher (who replaced one-dimensional lumbering sluggers with better all-around players). Thomson won the Giants' batting Triple Crown (.309/27/109) and led the team in hits, runs, doubles, and triples. In 1950 his average fell off, but Bobby still paced the team in homers and RBI. Then in '51, as the Giants won their first pennant since 1937, Thomson, playing third base to accommodate rookie Willie Mays in center field, hit .293 and a career-high 32 home runs.

With Mays serving in the army, the Giants finished second in '52 and fifth the next year, through no fault of Bobby Thomson. In '53 Bobby led the team in home runs for the fifth consecutive year and in RBI for the fourth time in five years; however, such consistent production was not enough to keep the three-time NL All-Star in Giants flannels. The team needed pitching and sent Thomson to the Milwaukee Braves in order to get left-hander Johnny Antonelli. The tall Scotsman promptly broke his ankle in spring training and played in only 43 games in 1954. He recovered enough to hit 20 homers for the Braves in '56, but he wasn't quite the same player, and Milwaukee traded him back to New York during the 1957 season. His last good season came with the Cubs in 1958.

Bobby Thomson was a very good player who stamped his name on the most dramatic moment in baseball history. There have been greater players, but few men have achieved such lasting legendary status with one history-shattering swing of the bat.

YEAR	TM	G	AB	R	H	HR	RBI	SB	BB	SO	AVG
1946–53, '57	NYG (9 yrs)	1135	4223	648	1171	189	704	31	360	477	.277
1954–57	MIL (4 yrs)	327	1041	121	252	38	168	6	97	183	.242
1958–59	CHC (2 yrs)	274	921	122	252	32	134	1	91	126	.274
1960	BOS (1 yr)	40	114	12	30	5	20	0	11	15	.263
1960	BAL (1 yr)	3	6	0	0	0	0	0	0	3	.000
Total (15 yrs)		1779	6305	903	1705	264	1026	38	559	804	.270

1951–1975

Monte Irvin

Before Willie Mays, there was Monte Irvin, the New York–San Francisco Giants' first standout African American player and one of the pioneers who followed right behind Jackie Robinson in the mission to desegregate the major leagues. The Haleburg, Alabama, native was the first black Giants' player to lead the National League in an important statistical category, the first black Giant to make the National League All-Star team (in 1952) and the first black Giant to be inducted into the National Baseball Hall of Fame. Furthermore, had World War II not interrupted the normal course of events, Irvin, and not Robinson, would most likely have been the first player to break the color line.

By 1942, when he was drafted into the United States Army, Monford Merrill Irvin (born February 25, 1919) had become one of the Negro League's brightest stars while playing for the Newark Eagles. Big, fast, possessed of a strong arm and powerful bat, Irvin could do it all on the ball diamond. An all-around schoolboy athlete, Irvin had earned 16 letters at East Orange (New Jersey) High School and had been all-state in four sports. This abundance of talent combined with his youth, unassailable character, and even temperament made him the consensus choice among Negro League team owners as the player best qualified to successfully integrate the white majors. The Dodgers' Branch Rickey agreed and after Irvin was discharged in 1945 made overtures about signing him to a Brooklyn contract.

Unfortunately, the war had dulled Irving's athletic abilities. He respected the cause of integration too much to risk failure, so he declined Rickey's offer in order to play himself back into top baseball shape. It didn't take long. That winter, he earned MVP honors in the Puerto Rican League and then led the Eagles to victory in the 1946 Negro League World Series, homering three times and scoring the winning run in Game 7.

Because of Rickey's reluctance to pay the Eagles for the rights to their star player, Irvin never did join the Dodgers. He became a New York Giant instead after owner Horace Stoneham paid the Eagles $5,000 for his contract. As a 30-year-old already past his prime, Irvin began his career in the Giants' organization with Jersey City of the International League. He was batting .373 when he was called to New York to make his major league debut as a pinch hitter on July 8, 1949.

Irvin didn't hit much in his 36-game trial in '49, but the following year, while playing first and the outfield, he began to shine like the veteran star he was, batting .299 with 15 home runs. He became the regular left fielder in 1951 when he made a major contribution to the Giants' historic pennant run with his mentoring of rookie Willie Mays and his own stellar performance: a .312 batting average with 24 home runs and a league-leading 121 RBI. Although the Giants lost to the Yankees, Irvin led all hitters in the World Series with a .458 average.

A broken ankle severely curtailed Irvin's season in 1952, and it bothered him the rest of his career, but he was still productive when reasonably healthy. He batted a career-high .329 in 124 games in 1953 with 21 home runs and 97 RBI, and he helped the Giants win another pennant in '54 by slugging 19 homers and knocking in 70 runs. After he began to slow down the next year, the Giants demoted him to Minneapolis and then traded him to Chicago, where he made one final decent showing in the white majors. His lifetime major league average of .293 paled in comparison to the .358 he averaged in the Negro Leagues, but it was more than enough to establish his credentials as an all-time great.

Irvin later worked for many years as Commissioner Bowie Kuhn's most trusted assistant and was universally admired as baseball's most genial ambassador. He was also elected to the baseball Halls of Fame of Mexico, Cuba, and Puerto Rico.

YEAR	TM	G	AB	R	H	HR	RBI	SB	BB	SO	AVG
1949–55	NYG (7 yrs)	653	2160	322	639	84	393	27	310	179	.296
1956	CHC (1 yr)	111	339	44	92	15	50	1	41	41	.271
Total (8 yrs)		764	2499	366	731	99	443	28	351	220	.293

Willie Mays

The greatest Giant of them all was an ebony Adonis from Birmingham, Alabama, who, as one early biographer succinctly put it, was "born to play ball." Willie Howard Mays played the game with an infectious joy that made him an instant media darling and the face of the franchise, a status he retains to this day. Called the "Say Hey Kid" because of the ebullient, high-pitched greeting he used as a rookie toward all the new faces whose names he couldn't remember, Mays was the quintessential five-tool player, and no one who saw him play has ever forgotten the vision of him on the diamond: pure baseball poetry in motion.

A natural if there ever was one, Mays inherited splendid physical gifts from his father, "Kitty Kat," who excelled on the steel mill teams of Birmingham. Even before graduating from high school, Mays served an intense apprenticeship in the Negro Leagues, so that the time he spent in the Giants' minor league system was more about acclimating him to integrated northern society than instruction on the finer points of the game.

Profane Giants manager Leo Durocher loved Mays at first sight and campaigned ceaselessly in early 1951 for his promotion to New York from Triple A. Giants owner Horace Stoneham did recall Mays but felt compelled to apologize in a full-page newspaper defense of the action to Minneapolis Millers fans, who had also come to love the youngster. The pressing Mays couldn't buy a hit his first week in the majors, but Durocher never doubted him and got him to relax by saying that Willie would be his center fielder no matter what. Mays's first major-league hit, a gargantuan home run off Warren Spahn, got him untracked and headed toward a .274/20/68 season in 121 games that merited him the NL Rookie of the Year Award.

The Giants, of course, won the 1951 pennant, and even though they lost the World Series to the Yankees, Mays faced for the first time the other great New York center fielder to whom he would be often compared: Mickey Mantle.

Willie lost the next two seasons to military service, and the Giants sank in the standings. When Durocher spied Mays's return in the spring of 1954, he predicted correctly, "Here comes the pennant." Mays hit .345 to win the NL batting title that year and earn his first of two NL MVP Awards, and his sensational over-the-shoulder catch of Vic Wertz's tee shot in Game 1 of the World Series set the stage for the Giants' sweep of the Indians, becoming the stuff of legend. For an encore the next year, Mays led the league in home runs with 51, establishing himself as the rare hitter who combines power and average. In all, Mays led the league in homers four times and batted over .300 ten times.

An automatic All-Star selection who played in a record 24 games, set several All-Star Game records, and won two All-Star Game MVP Awards, Mays demonstrated time and again over his 22-year career that there was nothing he couldn't do on a baseball diamond. He led the NL in stolen bases four straight years, despite running only when necessary to win a game, and he swiped a total of 338 bags.

As outstanding as Mays was in every other facet of the game, he may have been most brilliant on defense. Willie used his patented basket catch on routine flies, but he specialized in the spectacular. He made far too many great diving, long-running, and fence-climbing catches to enumerate, and he possessed one of the strongest, most accurate, most feared arms that ever hung off an outfielder. He owned the Gold Glove in his time and holds the career record for putouts and total chances by an outfielder.

Mays spent the twilight of his career back in New York with the Mets and became a first-ballot Hall of Famer in 1979. His legacy as baseball's greatest all-around player can be challenged by no one other than Babe Ruth.

YEAR	TM	G	AB	R	H	HR	RBI	SB	BB	SO	AVG
1951–52, '54–57	NYG (6 yrs)	762	2899	531	903	187	509	121	362	321	.312
1958–72	SFG (15 yrs)	2095	7578	1480	2284	459	1350	215	1032	1115	.301
1972–73	NYM (2 yrs)	135	404	51	96	14	44	2	70	90	.238
Total (22 yrs)		2992	10881	2062	3283	660	1903	338	1464	1526	.302

Mike McCormick

Without spending a day in the minor leagues, 17-year-old Mike McCormick found himself in the major leagues in 1956 as a bonus baby pitcher with the New York Giants. More than a decade later, after weathering much adversity, he became the first San Francisco Giant to win the Cy Young Award. His journey, as the Grateful Dead might have said, was a "long, strange trip," yet he enjoyed every minute of it, and he emerged as the winningest left-hander in the annals of San Francisco Giants baseball.

"Precocious" might have been a better middle name than his given one for Michael Francis McCormick, born September 29, 1938, in Pasadena, California. He began pitching American Legion ball at age 14 against high school juniors and seniors and dominated the competition with a tailing fastball, racking up a 49–4 record with four no-hitters. He was the highest-rated, most heavily scouted schoolboy pitcher in the Los Angeles area, with baseball-basketball scholarship offers from the University of Southern California and Stanford when, at age 17, he eloped and married his high school sweetheart.

Despite the buzz generated by the skinny California kid's blazing fastball, McCormick flew under the Giants' radar back east until he pitched in an exhibition at the Polo Grounds. Facing an All-Star team of New York State prepsters in front of a sellout crowd and Giants owner Horace Stoneham, Mike struck out all nine batters he faced. The Giants signed McCormick for $50,000, which meant under the existing rules that they had to keep him on the major league roster for two years. In his major league debut, on September 3, 1956, McCormick pitched a scoreless inning against the Phillies, inducing three routine grounders to second base.

After appearing in 27 games for the New York Giants, McCormick headed west as an original San Francisco Giant in 1958. Joining the starting rotation, he posted an 11–8 record with an ERA of 4.59. He cut half a point off his ERA in 1959 yet finished 12–16, due mostly to lack of run support and bad breaks. The next year, as a 21-year-old, he blossomed, turning in the second-best record (15–12) on the staff behind Sam Jones (18–14) and leading the National League in ERA with a mark of 2.70. Mike made the NL All-Star team that summer and the following year's squad (1961) as well.

Late in 1961, McCormick, who had been working out of the bullpen in addition to serving as the team's number one or number two starter, began experiencing arm problems. Pitching in pain, he was not as much of a factor in the Giants' drive to the 1962 pennant as expected—his biggest disappointment in baseball—and in December he was traded to the Baltimore Orioles in a six-player deal. Ineffective in Baltimore, McCormick pitched better for the woeful Washington Senators, winning 19 games in two seasons with ERAs below 3.50 both years, yet most observers thought he was washed up.

In a little-noticed December '66 trade with the Senators, the Giants reacquired their former prodigy, and he set about finally fulfilling his promise. Healthier and armed with a new screwball and improved curveball to supplement his somewhat shortened fastball, McCormick was a spot starter with a 4–3 record until he won a big game against Houston on June 13. He then went on a tear—winning eight straight, defeating the pennant-winning Cardinals three times, and finishing with a league-leading 22 victories and an ERA of 2.85. He won the NL Comeback Player of the Year Award in addition to the Cy Young.

Mike managed two more decent seasons with the Giants, but a chronic back injury hastened his demise as an effective hurler. After baseball he worked as a stockbroker and in the office-machine business. His Top Five rankings in wins, starts, complete games, shutouts, IP, and strikeouts assure his place in the San Francisco Giants' record book. His triumphant 1967 season has assured his legend.

YEAR	TM	W	L	ERA	GS	CG	SHO	IP	H	R	BB	SO
1956–57	NYG (2 yrs)	3	2	4.55	7	1	0	81.1	86	44	42	54
1958–62, '67–70	SFG (9 yrs)	104	94	3.64	245	77	19	1741.1	1651	789	574	976
1963–64	BAL (2 yrs)	6	10	4.41	23	2	0	153.1	153	80	74	88
1965–66	WAS (2 yrs)	19	22	3.42	53	11	4	374	351	162	87	189
1970	NYY (1 yr)	2	0	6.24	4	0	0	20.2	26	15	13	12
1971	KCR (1 yr)	0	0	9.78	1	0	0	9.2	14	10	5	2
Total (16 yrs)		134	128	3.73	333	91	23	2380.1	2281	1100	795	1321

Felipe Alou

Few Giants have had a greater impact on baseball and society than Felipe Alou. The talented outfielder from the Dominican Republic was the first of his countrymen to play regularly in the major leagues, he paved the way to San Francisco for his two younger brothers, and he did all he could to make straight the path of all Latin players in America. After his own fine playing career ended, he mentored scores of Latin youngsters as a minor league manager and then became the first Dominican manager of a major league team. His stint skippering the Giants made a perfect ending to a remarkable story.

Felipe Rojas Alou, born May 12, 1935, grew up in the small rural town of Haina, Dominican Republic. He had aspirations of becoming a doctor and signed with the Giants in 1955 primarily to help support his family. He experienced racial prejudice for the first time playing minor league ball in the United States but persevered and reached the majors halfway through the San Francisco Giants' inaugural (1958) season. It took him until 1961 to break out of a logjam in the Giants' outfield, when he batted .289 in 132 games. In 1962 he became the regular right fielder and a NL All-Star, hitting a team-high .316 with 25 home runs and 98 RBI. He played every inning of the World Series, going 7–26 against Yankees pitching.

After another good year (.281/20/82), Felipe was traded to the Milwaukee Braves. The Giants needed pitching help, and they were uncomfortable over Alou's outspokenness about the need for ML Baseball to do more to understand and help Latin players. In 1966 Felipe, who often batted leadoff, had his best year in baseball for the Braves, who by then had moved to Atlanta. He batted .327 with a career-high 31 homers and led the league in runs (122) and hits (218). He led the league in hits (210) again in 1968, while batting .317. He also made the All-Star team both seasons. At the end of his 17-year career, Alou was one of 31 players with 2,000+ hits, 200+ homers, and a lifetime average as high as his .286.

Matty Alou joined the Giants in 1960 and Jesus in 1963. Before Felipe was traded to Milwaukee, the three of them did something special. On September 15, 1963, they became the first brother trio in history to play together in the same outfield in a major league game. They also appeared in the same Giants' box scores of several other games. Matty, a diminutive left-handed slap hitter, later became a NL batting champion for Pittsburgh and hit .314 or better six times for the Pirates and Cardinals. Jesus, who spent most of his 15-year career with the Giants and the Houston Astros, played in 120+ games only four times, yet he still amassed 1,216 hits and recorded a lifetime average only six points lower than Felipe's .286.

In 1992, after a long minor league apprenticeship, Felipe was hired to manage a major league team, the Montreal Expos. Two years later, he was named NL Manager of the Year for leading the Expos to the best record (74–40) in major league baseball, prior to the season's premature end due to a players' strike. The Expos' leading hitter that summer was Felipe's 27-year-old son Moises Alou, who hit .339 with 22 homers.

Fired during his 11th season with the Expos, Felipe returned to San Francisco two years later to manage the 2003 Giants. He led the Giants to the NL West Division pennant that year with the second-best record (100–61) in all of baseball. His son Moises played for him once again in 2005 and '06 and batted over .300 both years. The Giants let Felipe go after the disappointing 2006 season, but San Franciscans cleave to their memories of him as the dashing Latin trailblazer who loved to play for them. In 2012, he became a special assistant to General Manager Brian Sabean.

YEAR	TM	G	AB	R	H	HR	RBI	SB	BB	SO	AVG
1958–63	SFG (6 yrs)	719	2292	337	655	85	325	51	138	308	.286
1964–65, '74	MIL (3 yrs)	267	973	140	270	32	129	13	61	106	.278
1966–69	ATL (4 yrs)	577	2378	324	719	62	206	27	127	180	.302
1970–71	OAK (2 yrs)	156	583	70	158	8	55	10	32	32	.271
1971–73	NYY (3 yrs)	344	1065	110	289	18	133	6	63	76	.271
1973	MON (1 yr)	19	48	4	10	1	4	0	2	4	.208
Total (17 yrs)		2082	7339	985	2101	206	852	107	423	706	.286

Orlando Cepeda

In the spring of 1957, when veteran New York–San Francisco Giants first baseman Whitey Lockman was mentoring his successor, a raw recruit from Puerto Rico named Orlando Cepeda, manager Bill Rigney asked Lockman for an update on his charge's progress.

"I think he might be three years away," said Lockman.

"Three years away from the major leagues?" cried an alarmed Rigney.

"No," replied Lockman. "From the Hall of Fame."

Cepeda did eventually earn a plaque in Cooperstown, but it wasn't as easy as Lockman joked it would be.

Born September 17, 1937, in Ponce, Puerto Rico, Orlando Manuel Cepeda grew up in the shadow of his father, Pedro, a great baseball star in his native country. A power-hitting shortstop and friend of Negro League legends Satchel Paige and Josh Gibson, Pedro was known as "The Bull" for his strength, volatile temper, and fierce pride. Overweight and intimidated by the stature of his famous father, Orlando favored basketball as a youngster but returned to baseball when the baby fat melted into muscle and he started hitting the baseball a long way. When asked if his son would ever be as good a baseball player as he was, Pedro said, "No. He will be better."

Caribbean bird dog Pete Zorilla convinced the Giants to sign Cepeda for $500 out of a tryout camp in Melbourne, Florida, but Orlando's inability to speak English, his loneliness, and the racial prejudice he faced almost ended his professional baseball career in the low minors. Cepeda's 1956 win of the Northern League's Triple Crown for St. Cloud (Minnesota) caused the Giants to finally take him seriously. After Orlando had another good year in Triple A, the Giants gave him the starting first baseman's job. In the first game in San Francisco Giants history, in only his second major league at bat,

the confident 20-year-old blasted a home run against the Dodgers at Seals Stadium, immediately igniting a love affair between himself and San Franciscans.

Cepeda went on to win the NL Rookie of the Year Award—for batting .312 with a league-leading 38 doubles, 25 homers, and 96 RBI—and Giants fans voted him the team MVP, ahead of the more deserving Willie Mays. The next year Cepeda improved to .317/27/105, establishing himself as one of the game's rising stars, and he made the NL All-Star team for the first of six consecutive seasons with the Giants.

"The Baby Bull," as Cepeda began to be known, had his best year ever in San Francisco in 1961 when he led the NL in HR (46) and a team-record 142 RBI, while batting .311. He averaged 33 HR and 103 RBI the next three years while hitting over .300 each season, but a chronic knee problem limited him to 33 games in 1965 and, along with the Giants' decision to go with Willie McCovey at first base, led to his trade to St. Louis the following season.

Giants fans, who'd come to adore the outgoing, fun-loving Cepeda, were hardly surprised when he led the Cardinals to NL pennants in 1967 and '68, winning the 1967 NL MVP Award along the way. He helped Atlanta win its first Divisional Championship in 1969 and finished his career DH-ing for Boston and Kansas City. In 1973 he won the Designated Hitter of the Year Award. Cepeda retired as the Latin American career home-run champ with 379, and he remains ranked among the Top Ten in almost every San Francisco Giants batting category.

A repentant Cepeda worked hard to restore his good name after a conviction for minor marijuana smuggling, and he was rewarded with a well-deserved and overdue election to the Baseball Hall of Fame in 1999. He proudly serves the Giants today as a community ambassador.

YEAR	TM	G	AB	R	H	HR	RBI	SB	BB	SO	AVG
1958–66	SFG (9 yrs)	1114	4178	652	1286	226	767	92	259	636	.308
1966–68	STL (3 yrs)	431	1615	227	469	58	242	28	139	239	.290
1969–72	ATL (4 yrs)	401	1474	198	414	74	252	21	131	197	.281
1972	OAK (1 yr)	3	3	0	0	0	0	0	0	0	.000
1973	BOS (1 yr)	142	550	51	159	20	86	0	50	81	.289
1974	KCR (1 yr)	33	107	3	23	1	18	1	9	16	.215
Total (17 yrs)		2124	7927	1131	2351	379	1365	142	588	1169	.297

Jim Davenport

If anyone could be said to "bleed Giant Orange," it would be Jim Davenport, an "organization" man if the Giants ever had one. James Houston Davenport not only spent his entire 13-year major league playing career with the Giants, he has served the franchise in various capacities for more than 50 years, along the way becoming a true San Francisco Giants legend and one of the most popular figures in franchise history.

Born August 17, 1933, in Siluria, Alabama, Davenport went to Mississippi Southern University (now Southern Mississippi) on a football scholarship and helped lead the team to back-to-back Sun Bowl appearances in 1953 and '54. He signed with the Giants in 1955, and his glove was so good he beat out the better-hitting veteran Ray Jablonski for the third baseman's job in 1958, the Giants' first year in San Francisco. Giants manager Bill Rigney called him "the greatest third baseman I ever saw." Jim batted .256 with 12 home runs and made *The Sporting News* All-Rookie Team.

Davenport became a fixture at the hot corner in San Francisco for almost a decade, while a succession of players manned the position for the Giants' despised West Coast rivals, the Los Angeles Dodgers. Blessed with soft hands and an accurate arm, Jim led NL third basemen in fielding percentage three times (1959–61) and won a Gold Glove Award in 1962. He set a major league record for consecutive errorless games at third (97) that was not broken until 1999.

A career .258 hitter, Davenport tried to maximize his abilities with the bat by doing the little things, such as sacrifice bunting and hitting behind the runner. He was also a clutch hitter, with a lifetime batting average of .285 with runners in scoring position and .338 with a runner on third and less than two out. He hit .290 against the toughest pitcher of his time, Sandy Koufax. His best year at the plate came in 1962, when he hit .297 with 14 home runs. He drew a bases-loaded walk, forcing in the winning run in the playoff game against the Dodgers that clinched the 1962 pennant for the Giants, and he tied a record by turning four double plays in the World Series against the Yankees. Davvy made the NL All-Star team that summer and singled off Cleveland's Dick Donovan in his only at bat to help the Senior Circuit win the game played in Washington, D.C., 3–1.

Davenport's contributions went beyond what he did with bat and glove. While he did not consciously attempt to facilitate racial harmony on the Giants team, he did much to bring it about just by being himself. Willie Mays and Willie McCovey admired him as much as he admired them, and his close friendship with Bobby Bonds, in particular, did not go unnoticed. He never grumbled about playing a supporting role on a team full of stars, and as his career wound down he mentored a number of younger players, including a couple in line to take his place.

Davenport began his post-playing career by managing the Giants' Triple-A farm club in Phoenix for three years (1971–73). In addition to stints coaching for San Diego, Philadelphia, and Cleveland and scouting for Detroit, Jim has served the Giants for decades as a scout, instructor, coach, and manager in both the major and minor leagues. In 1985 the fans voted him third baseman of the San Francisco Giants' 25th anniversary Dream Team, and the 1,130 games he played at third remain the most ever by a Giant.

YEAR	TM	G	AB	R	H	HR	RBI	SB	BB	SO	AVG
1958–70	SFG (13 yrs)	1501	4427	552	1142	77	456	16	382	673	.258

Willie McCovey

"If you pitch to him, he'll ruin baseball. He'd hit 80 home runs." So said Cincinnati Reds manager Sparky Anderson to explain why he and his National League colleagues were intentionally walking Giants first baseman Willie McCovey a record 45 times during the summer of 1969. Anderson may have been exaggerating, but not by much. Despite the care with which he was pitched to, "Stretch" led the league in home runs (45), RBI (126), on-base percentage (.458), and slugging percentage (.656) and batted .320 to win the NL MVP Award, proving, as Sparky had implied, that the 6'4", 230-pound McCovey was the most intimidating and dangerous batter in the league.

The summer of '69, when McCovey blasted two home runs in the All-Star Game and was named the winner of the contest's MVP Award, was the height of "Big Mac"-phobia all right. But pitchers had been trembling at the sight of the howitzer shots launched noisily off the powerful left-hander's bat for a decade—ever since Willie's major league debut on July 30, 1959, when he went 4–4 with a pair of singles and a pair of triples off Robin Roberts, a Hall of Fame pitcher. McCovey, who strung together a 22-game hitting streak and batted .354 overall, was so impressive that he won the NL Rookie of the Year Award despite playing in only 52 games that season.

Amazingly, McCovey's Hall of Fame career, highlighted by his 521 home runs, would have been even more remarkable had it not been for two impediments. Bad feet and injuries to both knees hobbled McCovey throughout his career, and the presence of Orlando Cepeda, another natural first baseman, limited McCovey's playing time during his first four years with the Giants and caused him to be played out of position, in the outfield, a couple of more years. In the pennant-winning year of 1962 Willie played 91 games and only 17 of them at first base. The screaming line drive he hit to Yankees second baseman

Bobby Richardson to end the seventh game of the World Series is one of the most famous outs in baseball history.

McCovey did not get the regular first base job until 1965, and the Giants did not completely resolve the situation until May 8, 1966, when they traded Cepeda to the St. Louis Cardinals.

The years 1963–70 were the prime of McCovey's 19-year tenure in San Francisco. Over those eight seasons, the big guy from Mobile, Alabama (born January 10, 1938), averaged 36 homers and drove in 90+ runs seven times. He led the National League in homers three times, RBI twice, and slugging percentage three consecutive years (1968–70). And he did all this clouting in an era when the dominance of pitching led to rules changes to boost hitting.

In 1971, another knee injury limited McCovey to 105 games, yet he made the All-Star team for the sixth and final time, and he had a good NLCS against the Pirates, going 6–14 with two home runs. A broken arm curtailed his 1972 season to only 81 games. He bounced back to blast 29 homers in '73, but the Giants, in the midst of a salary dump, then traded him to San Diego.

After two decent years for the Padres, McCovey lost his job to a younger player and was sold to the Oakland A's, who released him after the 1976 season. With no guarantees, McCovey made the Giants' roster out of spring training the following year. The long standing ovation he received on Opening Day cemented his emotional ties to the franchise and the city and inspired the performance (.280/28/86) that led to his winning the NL Comeback of the Year Award. The Giants have honored this beloved member of the family in numerous ways, most notably by inaugurating the award that bears his name in 1980 and by redubbing the inlet behind AT&T Park "McCovey Cove."

YEAR	TM	G	AB	R	H	HR	RBI	SB	BB	SO	AVG
1959–73, '77–80	SFG (19 yrs)	2256	7214	1113	1974	469	1388	24	1168	1351	.274
1974–76	SDP (3 yrs)	321	959	116	232	52	167	2	174	195	.242
1976	OAK (1 yr)	11	24	0	5	0	0	0	3	4	.208
Total (22 yrs)		2588	8197	1229	2211	521	1555	26	1345	1550	.270

Juan Marichal

The Giants' Latin American connection has paid many splendid dividends over the years but none so profitable as the acquisition of the services of a poor farm lad from the Dominican Republic named Juan Antonio Sanchez Marichal. A right-handed pitcher with an iconic windup and pinpoint control, Marichal won more games (151) than any other pitcher in the National League in the 1960s. With Marichal on the mound and Willie Mays in center field, the San Francisco Giants took the field every fourth day for many years with baseball's best player and best pitcher in their lineup.

From a very young age, Marichal was determined to become a major leaguer. As unlikely as that outcome was for someone in Juan's circumstances, his talent was impossible to miss. He rose like a rocket through the amateur ranks until he was coerced into pitching for the Dominican dictator's Aviacion (air force) team. Soon afterward he signed with the professional Escogido Lions, who immediately sold him to the Giants for $1, to give him a shot at his dream. Marichal's ascent through the minors was just as swift, and two and a half years after coming to America he made a spectacular major league debut (on July 19, 1960), pitching a complete game, one-hit shutout (with 12 Ks) against Philadelphia.

The rest of the NL quickly discovered what the Phillies were the first to find out: that Juan had all the pitches, including a devastating screwball and change-of-pace, plus the rare ability to locate those pitches as if they were guided by radar. His unorthodox kicking-the-sky, seesaw delivery made him even tougher to hit, as it helped him disguise his pitches until the last moment.

Marichal went 6–2 as a rookie and then embarked on one of the most consistently outstanding careers ever turned in by a Giants pitcher. He won in double figures 12 times in the next 13 years (1961–73) and won more than 20 games six times in a seven-year stretch; with highs of 25 in 1963 and 26 in '68 (both were league-leading totals). He pitched 200 or more innings 11 times, and in three of those seasons he worked more than 300 innings. He compiled an ERA under 2.50 six times, with lows of 2.13 in 1965 and a league-leading 2.10 in '69. He struck out at least 150 batters nine times, and in six of those years his strikeout total topped 200.

As tough as he was to hit, the "Dominican Dandy" was even stingier with the free pass. Juan walked only 709 batters in his 16-year career, against 2,303 strikeouts, for a strikeout-to-walk ratio of 3.25—one of the best marks in history.

Marichal made the All-Star team ten times and pitched a no-hitter against the Astros on June 15, 1963. He pitched four scoreless innings in the 1962 World Series but had to come out of Game Four after injuring his hand while bunting in the top of the fifth. And, in one of the most famous pitching duels of all time, he threw a 16-inning shutout against the Braves on July 2, 1963, to beat the ageless Warren Spahn 1–0 on a home run by Willie Mays.

Friendly and well-liked, Marichal nevertheless was a no-nonsense competitor on the mound—unafraid to pitch inside, especially against the Giants' bitter rivals, the Dodgers. That intensity bore disastrous results during the 1965 NL pennant race when Marichal, enraged that Dodgers' catcher John Roseboro threw a return pitch too close to his head, clubbed Roseboro over the head with his bat. While Roseboro did not suffer serious injury, the incident marred Marichal's image and even delayed his election to the Baseball Hall of Fame until Roseboro, who had long before forgiven and befriended Juan, spoke out on his behalf.

The holder of numerous San Francisco records that will never be broken, Marichal entered the Halls of Cooperstown in 1983. A bronze statue of him in his famous delivery stands outside AT&T Park.

YEAR	TM	W	L	ERA	GS	CG	SHO	IP	H	R	BB	SO
1960–73	SFG (14 yrs)	238	140	2.84	446	244	52	3443.2	3081	1288	690	2281
1974	BOS (1 yr)	5	1	4.89	9	0	0	57.1	61	32	14	21
1975	LAD (1 yr)	0	1	13.50	2	0	0	6	11	9	5	1
Total (16 yrs)		243	142	2.89	457	244	52	3507	3153	1329	709	2303

Gaylord Perry

After being outbid for high school pitching phenom Tony Cloninger in the spring of 1958, the Giants settled for another promising arm out of North Carolina tobacco country, a strapping good ol' boy named Gaylord Jackson Perry, who turned out to be not only one of the team's most fascinating characters but also one of the greatest hurlers in the history of the game.

Born September 15, 1938, into an industrious tenant-farming family, the right-handed Gaylord was the younger brother of Jim Perry, who preceded Gaylord into pro ball and eventually won 215 major league games. A natural athlete and three-sport star at Williamston (North Carolina) High School, the 6'4", 215-pound younger Perry had big league pitcher written all over him. He broke into the majors at the end of his fifth season in the minors, going 3–1 in 13 games for the '62 Giants.

Despite zip on his fastball, a decent curve, and good control, Perry had trouble breaking into the Giants' starting rotation, so in the summer of 1964 he talked veteran pitcher Bob Shaw into teaching him how to throw the spitball (an illegal and difficult pitch to control that drops sharply). Two years later Perry had mastered the wet one, becoming the second ace of the Giants' staff (behind Juan Marichal) as well as a frustrating, maddening enigma for NL batters and umpires to contend with. He earned his first of four All-Star team selections in 1966, and his 21–8 record (with an ERA of 2.99) was his first of five 20+ win seasons.

Gaylord was a workhorse for the rest of his career in San Francisco, twice leading the NL in IP, averaging 303 IP a year (for five years), and establishing the San Francisco season record for IP in 1970 with 329. He pitched a 1–0 no-hitter against the St. Louis Cardinals on September 17, 1968, and turned in sterling ERAs of 2.44 and 2.49 in '68 and '69, but his best overall year for the Giants may have come in 1970 when he went 23–13 and reeled off four straight shutouts and 40 consecutive scoreless innings.

Perry learned to drive the opposition crazy with his constant fidgeting—he seemed to touch every part of his body and uniform before each pitch—and the mere threat of the spitball, and later the Vaseline ball, became almost as effective a weapon as the pitch itself.

(Perry once said his goal was to lead the league each year in psych-outs.) Batters and opposing managers complained about him continually, but umpires were never able to find any evidence of his cheating, despite their frequent and often comic checks of his clothing and person. Ironically, Perry admitted his guilt in his 1974 autobiography, *Me and the Spitter,* although he enjoyed using euphemisms such as "super sinker" or "hard slider" in referring to the illegal pitches he insists he never threw.

Traded after the 1971 season for younger southpaw Sam McDowell, Perry departed with 134 wins, which remains the second most in San Francisco Giants' history. He went on to rack up an amazing 180 more wins for seven different teams over 12 years. He went 24–16 with a 1.92 ERA to win the 1972 American League Cy Young Award in his first year with Cleveland, a fifth-place team, and two years later won 21 for the Tribe. When he went 21–6 in 1978 at age 40 for the San Diego Padres, he won a second Cy Young Award, becoming the first pitcher to win the award in both leagues.

He won his 300th game for Seattle in 1982 and is one of only seven pitchers with 300 wins and more than 3,500 strikeouts. Voted into the National Baseball Hall of Fame in 1991, he remains ranked second in seven career categories among San Francisco Giants pitchers.

YEAR	TM	W	L	ERA	GS	CG	SHO	IP	H	R	BB	SO
1962–71	SFG (10 yrs)	134	109	2.96	283	125	21	2294.2	2061	892	581	1606
1972–75	CLE (4 yrs)	70	57	2.71	133	96	17	1130.2	918	377	330	773
1975–77, '80	TEX (4 yrs)	48	43	3.26	112	55	12	827.1	787	345	190	575
1978–79	SDP (2 yrs)	33	17	2.88	69	15	2	493.1	466	186	133	294
1980	NYY (1 yr)	4	4	4.48	8	0	0	50.2	65	33	18	28
1981	ATL (1 yr)	8	9	3.95	23	3	0	150.2	182	70	24	60
1982–83	SEA (2 yrs)	13	22	4.58	48	8	0	318.2	361	177	77	158
1983	KCR (1 yr)	4	4	4.28	14	1	1	84.1	98	48	26	40
Total (22 yrs)		314	265	3.11	690	303	53	5350.1	4938	2128	1379	3534

Bobby Bonds

In the beginning, he was overshadowed by his hero. In the prime of his ascendancy, he was dogged by the curse of "unfulfilled potential." And in the end, his fame has been obscured by his own son's achievements. No, this is not the plot of an Elizabethan tragedy but the sad arc of the career of Bobby Lee Bonds, one of the unique and most exciting talents in the history of the San Francisco Giants.

From birth (March 15, 1946, in Riverside, California) Bobby Bonds was destined for athletic greatness. An older brother played pro football for the Kansas City Chiefs, while his older sister was an Olympic hurdler. A four-sport star in high school, Bobby was named Southern California Schoolboy Athlete of the Year in 1964. After two-and-a-half seasons in the Giants' farm system, Bonds made a spectacular ML debut while playing next to his idol Willie Mays: in his very first game he blasted a grand-slam home run at Candlestick against the reviled Dodgers on June 25, 1968. He played in 81 games as a rookie, batting .254 with nine home runs.

The next year, in his first full season, the rangy right fielder demonstrated the rare combination of abilities—burning speed and tremendous power—that made him such a spectacular player. Bonds hit 32 home runs and swiped 45 bases, becoming just the fourth 30–30 player (along with Ken Williams, Mays, and Hank Aaron) in history. He would go on to notch a total of five 30–30 seasons (a record since tied by his son Barry), and he remains the only player other than Alfonso Soriano to accomplish the feat in both leagues. Because of his speed, Bonds batted much of his career from the lead-off spot, from which he hit record numbers of home runs: 11 leadoff HR in 1973 and 35 in his career.

Unfortunately, Bonds's Achilles' heel also manifested itself in 1969, as he struck out a record 187 times. A year later, he whiffed 189 times, and the strikeout would mar his résumé and reputation throughout his career. Bonds modeled himself after his hero, and his devotion to his mentor fueled expectations that he would become the "next Willie Mays"—an impossible burden for any player.

Nevertheless, after the 1972 trade of Mays to the Mets, Bonds assumed the Giants' leadership mantle. He made the NL All-Star team in 1971 and in 1973 when the NL skipper, Reds manager Sparky Anderson, called him "the best player in baseball today." Bonds backed up the assertion by homering and doubling to win the MVP Award of the '73 exhibition. Bonds had his best overall year for San Francisco in '73, when he hit .283, scored 131 runs, drove in 96 runs, stole 43 bases, and slammed a career-high 39 homers.

Bonds's drinking problem and off year in 1974 caused the Giants to trade him to the New York Yankees for Bobby Murcer; this was the first trade of $100,000 superstars in history. Bobby proved he could still play by putting together another 30–30 season and making the 1975 American League All-Star team, but the trade to the Yankees started a career decline, in which he played for six different ball clubs in his final six seasons. After hanging 'em up, Bonds coached for the Indians and Giants, served as vice president of the MLB Players' Alumni Association, and followed the exploits of his son Barry.

Bobby Bonds never measured up to his hero, but he did enough in his seven-year stint with the San Francisco Giants to plant his name throughout the team's record book (he is listed in eight of the 12 Top Ten batting categories). He is tied for first in stolen bases (263) with Barry, and he and Barry are also the top father-son HR duo of all time.

YEAR	TM	G	AB	R	H	HR	RBI	SB	BB	SO	AVG
1968–74	SFG (7 yrs)	1014	4047	765	1106	186	552	263	500	1016	.273
1975	NYY (1 yr)	145	529	93	143	32	85	30	89	137	.270
1976–77	CAL (2 yrs)	257	970	151	256	47	169	71	115	231	.264
1978	CWS (1 yr)	26	90	8	25	2	8	6	10	10	.278
1978	TEX (1 yr)	130	475	85	126	29	82	37	69	110	.265
1979	CLE (1 yr)	146	538	93	148	25	85	34	74	135	.275
1980	STL (1 yr)	86	231	37	47	5	24	15	33	74	.203
1981	CHC (1 yr)	45	163	26	35	6	19	5	24	44	.215
Total (14 yrs)		1849	7043	1258	1886	332	1024	461	914	1757	.268

Jack Clark

One of the most feared sluggers in the National League, Jack Anthony Clark was the shining star who helped Giants fans survive the dismal days of the early 1980s. No matter how poorly the team was doing, when Clark manned right field at Candlestick there was a reason to go to the ballgame.

A Pennsylvania native, Clark (born November 10, 1955, in New Brighton) was the mound ace of his high school team in Azusa, California, who attracted scouts' attention with his blazing fastball. After signing with the Giants as the team's 13th pick in the 1973 free-agent draft and converting to the outfield, he blew through the San Francisco farm system, arriving for cups of coffee at the end of the 1975 and '76 seasons. The next year he appeared in 136 games and hit 13 HR with 51 RBI to win a place on *Baseball Digest*'s Rookie All-Star team.

He came into his own in 1978, playing in 156 games and batting .306. He led the team in hits (181), runs (90), HR (25), and RBI (90), and his 46 doubles set a San Francisco Giants record that stood until 2001, when Jeff Kent hit 49. He also made his first All-Star team and put together a 26-game hitting streak, which remains the franchise record.

The 6'3", 205-pound Clark, with his impatient bat waggle and the trademark lampblack smears under his eyes, was an imposing sight in the batter's box, and he never got cheated while taking his fierce cuts at the baseball. A dead-pull hitter, "Jack the Ripper" was the Giants' most consistent power threat during his tenure with the team, and he led San Francisco in HR, RBI, and runs four times each. An adequate fielder, Clark possessed a cannon, which he used to finish first in the league in assists in 1981. In 1983 he threw out 17 base runners, including

five at home. He made the All-Star team again in 1979 and had another good year in 1980 (.284/22/82), despite missing more than a month of the season because of a broken hand—the first of several injuries that would nag him for the rest of his career. Clark was also at his best in the clutch. He led the league in GWRBI (18) in 1980, set the current team seasonal record for GWRBI in 1982 with 21, and after the 1983 season was the NL career leader in the category, which officially began in 1979.

In 1982 Clark had his final big year (.274/27/103) in San Francisco, becoming the first Giant since 1971 to drive in 100 or more runs. He became discontented with Candlestick Park and the team's lack of competitiveness, and after a knee injury limited him to 57 games in 1984 the Giants granted his wish and traded him in early 1985 to the St. Louis Cardinals for four players.

Clark became a first baseman in St. Louis, made the All-Star team in 1985 and '87, and led the Cardinals to pennants both years. In '87 he led the league in walks, on-base percentage, and slugging percentage, and his 35 home runs and 106 RBI were both career highs. His three-run home run against the Dodgers in Game 6 of the NLCS clinched the '87 pennant for the Cards.

Unable to find a situation that suited him, Clark spent the next four years bouncing from the Yankees to the Padres to the Red Sox, despite averaging 27 HR and 84 RBI per year. He retired in 1992 after playing 81 games for Boston. He wore several ML uniforms, but Silver Anniversary Dream Team right fielder Jack Clark will always be a San Francisco Giant. Only Willie Mays, Bobby Bonds, and Barry Bonds played more games in the San Francisco outfield than he.

YEAR	TM	G	AB	R	H	HR	RBI	SB	BB	SO	AVG
1975–84	SFG (10 yrs)	1044	3731	597	1034	163	595	60	497	556	.277
1985–87	STL (3 yrs)	322	1093	198	299	66	216	3	264	288	.274
1988	NYY (1 yr)	150	496	81	120	27	93	3	113	141	.242
1989–90	SDP (2 yrs)	257	789	135	199	51	156	10	236	236	.252
1991–92	BOS (2 yrs)	221	738	107	174	33	120	1	152	220	.236
Total (18 yrs)		1994	6847	1118	1826	340	1180	77	1262	1441	.267

Will Clark

When the 22-year-old first baseman Will Clark batted for the first time in the major leagues on April 8, 1986, he didn't just make a good impression. He made a sensational debut by homering off Nolan Ryan, one of fastest, most intimidating pitchers in baseball history. Giants' fans knew right then and there that Will "The Thrill" would live up to the hype.

Born March 13, 1964, in New Orleans, Louisiana, William Nuschler Clark wasn't really a home-run hitter, although he finished his 15-year career with 284 long balls, 176 of them coming when he was wearing the black and orange. He was instead a "pure" hitter with power, the possessor of a left-handed swing so perfect and beautiful that he was considered a natural.

An All-American in both high school and college, Clark played for the famous Ron Polk at Mississippi State University, where he and teammate Rafael Palmeiro became known as "Thunder and Lightning." In 1984 he starred on the U.S. Olympic team alongside Barry Larkin and Mark McGwire, batting .429 with three home runs and eight RBI in five games. Clark won the 1985 Golden Spikes Award (given to the country's best collegiate baseball player), and the Giants took him as the second overall pick of the June Free Agent draft. He played in only 65 minor league games and 10 instructional league contests before becoming the Giants' starting first baseman. Rising again to the occasion, Clark homered off Houston's Bob Knepper on April 15 in his first game in Candlestick Park. An elbow injury limited him to 111 games in '86, his rookie year, but he still managed to bat .287 while helping the Giants finish third in the old NL West Division and become only the ninth team since 1900 to compile a winning record after losing 100 or more games the year before.

In 1987, "The Thrill" showed what he could do over a full season, batting .308 with 35 home runs and 91 RBI in 150 games. He tied a San Francisco record with RBI in nine straight games, became the seventh Giant to post a .300/30 HR season, and finished fifth in the NL MVP balloting. The following year he played in all 162 of the Giants' games (becoming only the second player in San Francisco history to play every game in a season), and his teammates voted him MVP of the team. He led the NL in RBI (109), walks (100), and intentional walks (27) and made his first NL All-Star team, becoming the first San Francisco player since shortstop Chris Speier to start the game. He also batted .360 in the Giants' first postseason series (a seven-game defeat to St. Louis) since 1971.

Clark put his stamp on Giants history in 1989 when he led the team to its first World Series since 1962. He hit .333 to finish second in the NL batting race, was ranked among the leaders in nearly all other batting categories, won the first of his two Silver Slugger Awards, and placed second in the NL MVP balloting. More importantly, he carried the Giants to victory over the Cubs in the NLCS—earning MVP honors for batting .650 with three home runs, including two off Greg Maddux in Game 1. He enjoyed one more productive season (.301/29/116) for San Francisco in 1991, when he also won the Gold Glove Award.

A free agent after the 1993 season, Clark played seven more years—for Texas, Baltimore, and St. Louis. He finished with 2,176 hits, 1,205 RBI, and a lifetime average of .303. He was inducted into the College Baseball Hall of Fame in 2006 and today serves the Giants as a community ambassador, proud that his name appears in the Top Ten list of every significant San Francisco Giants batting category.

YEAR	TM	G	AB	R	H	HR	RBI	SB	BB	SO	AVG
1986–93	SFG (8 yrs)	1160	4269	687	1278	176	709	52	506	744	.299
1994–98	TEX (5 yrs)	609	2226	381	686	77	397	8	324	335	.308
1999–2000	BAL (2 yrs)	156	507	89	153	19	57	6	85	87	.302
2000	STL (1 yr)	51	171	29	59	12	42	1	22	24	.345
Total (15 yrs)		1976	7173	1186	2176	284	1205	67	937	1190	.303

Matt Williams

The best advice Matt Williams ever got came when he needed it most. In 1989, after the discouraged Williams was shuttled between Phoenix and San Francisco for the third year in a row, his father told him, "Make 'em rip the jersey off you. If you quit, you'll never know if you'd been good enough." The redetermined player not only became the best third baseman in franchise history, he also, if not for injuries, would have become—in the opinion of former Giants' general manager Al Rosen, who made him the team's number 1 pick of the 1986 draft—the greatest all-around third sacker in baseball history.

The Giants scouted Williams while he was playing at the University of Nevada, Las Vegas, and after watching how the other players gravitated toward him during pregame activities, Rosen became convinced that Matt was a natural-born leader. Even though Williams batted only .202 in '89 during his third shot with the Giants, the team never lost faith in him. The 18 major league homers he hit in 84 games, combined with the 26 he hit in Phoenix, gave him the second most in all of professional baseball that year and indicated the power production he was capable of. Matt also helped the Giants defeat Chicago in the NLCS, lighting up Cubs' pitchers for two homers and nine RBI.

With the help of batting coach Dusty Baker, who got him to lay off curves in the dirt, Williams finally established himself as a regular in 1990, hitting 33 home runs in 159 games and knocking in 122 runs, a franchise record for third basemen. He was named to the NL All-Star team and would make the squad three more times as a Giant.

An intense, no-nonsense competitor who seldom laughed or smiled on the diamond, Williams was a workaholic who was given the moniker "The Big

Marine" for his toughness. While he intimidated opponents with his deadpan glare, he became a fan favorite and, as Rosen had expected, a team bellwether who led by quiet example. Teaming up first with Will Clark and then with Barry Bonds, he anchored the middle of the Giants' lineup. He also played stellar defense, winning Gold Gloves in 1991, '93, and '94.

Williams slugged 38 homers in 1993 and the next year was on a pace to hit 62 and become the first player to break Roger Maris's single-season home-run record when the season ended August 11 because of the players' strike. The 43 homers he did hit in 112 games became his career high. Injuries limited him to 76 and 105 games the next two seasons and contributed to the Giants' very unpopular decision to trade him to Cleveland for four players. Williams departed ranked fourth in home runs and fifth in RBI in the all-time rankings for San Francisco Giants batters.

Williams hit 32 homers and drove in 105 runs to help the Indians get to the World Series in 1997, but he asked for and was granted a trade to the expansion Arizona Diamondbacks after the season so he could live close to his children in Phoenix. His six-year run with the D-Backs concluded his playing career. His final big year came in 1999, when he made his fifth All-Star team, batting .303 with 35 home runs and a career-high 190 hits and 142 RBI. He finally became a World Series champion when Arizona beat the Yankees in the 2001 Fall Classic, and by homering in Game 2 he became the only player to hit a World Series home run for three different teams.

After hanging up his spikes, Williams worked in the Arizona front office and broadcast booth before serving as a Diamondbacks coach under manager Kirk Gibson. In 2014 he managed the Washington Nationals to the NL Eastern Division pennant in his first year at the helm.

YEAR	TM	G	AB	R	H	HR	RBI	SB	BB	SO	AVG
1987–96	SFG (10 yrs)	1120	4139	594	1092	247	732	29	272	872	.264
1997	CLE (1 yr)	151	596	86	157	32	105	12	34	108	.264
1998–2003	ARZ (6 yrs)	595	2265	317	629	99	381	12	163	383	.278
Total (17 yrs)		1866	7000	997	1878	378	1218	53	469	1363	.268

Barry Bonds

While the numerous records of Barry Bonds are astonishing to behold, it is impossible to ignore the conditions under which he set them. It is truly a shame that his is not a simple story of baseball greatness but a cautionary tale of jealousy, arrogance, unbridled ambition, and dishonesty. On a strictly numerical and statistical basis, Barry Bonds can be regarded as one of the greatest players in baseball history. Yet, in the collective consciousness of the baseball fan, he stands not alongside the cherished elites of the game such as Babe Ruth, Willie Mays, and Hank Aaron but next to tarnished stars such as Shoeless Joe Jackson, Pete Rose, and the other standouts of the performance-enhancing-drugs era.

Born July 24, 1964, in Riverside, California, Bonds was destined to leave his mark on the national pastime. Blessed with great physical gifts inherited from his father Bobby and tutored from an early age by his godfather, Willie Mays, and other San Francisco Giants, Barry always seemed too advanced for the competition he faced in high school and at Arizona State University. The number 1 pick of the Pittsburgh Pirates in the 1985 draft, he played only 115 games in the minors before getting the call in May 1986. Despite batting .223 in 113 games, he led National League rookies in homers, RBI, stolen bases, and walks.

Barry showed flashes of brilliance over the next three years and then began to fulfill his enormous potential. He won the NL MVP Award in 1990 with a fine performance (.301/33/114 plus 52 stolen bases), finished second in the MVP race the following year, and then won his second MVP Award in three years in 1992. That year he batted .311 with 34 homers and 103 RBI and led the league in on-base percentage, slugging percentage, runs, walks, and intentional walks.

The slender, sinewy Bonds had become the superb all-around player his father never quite did: a versatile, dangerous hitter; a Gold Glove left fielder; and one of the leading base stealers in the game. Somehow, it wasn't enough. Bonds underperformed in three NLCS with the Pirates, spent time in manager Jim Leyland's doghouse, and fled the Steel City in December of '92 to sign with the Giants as a free agent.

As a Giant, Bonds immediately took his game to a new level. He batted .336 and led the league in homers (46) and RBI (123), achieving career highs in all three categories. He also won his third NL MVP Award. Barry was annually brilliant the next seven years: smashing 40+ homers a year three times, hitting over .300 four times, driving in 100+ runs five times, and leading the league in walks five times. It was only a warm-up for the climax of his career: four MVP seasons in a row (2001–04), an incredible run, which gave him an unprecedented seven such awards.

In 2001 the beefed-up Bonds obliterated the major league single-season home-run record by blasting 73 long balls, while setting the major league record for slugging percentage (.863). The next year he batted .370 to become only the fourth Giant ever to win a NL batting title. Then, after another merely outstanding season in 2003 (.341/45/90 in 130 games), Bonds erupted for his final great season in '04. He hit .362 to win his second batting title and set major league records for on-base percentage (.609), walks (232), and intentional walks (120).

In the 2002 World Series, Bonds finally redeemed his previous poor postseason performances by batting .471 with four homers against the Anaheim Angels. The crowning achievement of his career came on August 7, 2007, in his final season, when he hit home run number 756, making him the all-time major league home-run leader. No player not already a member of the National Hall of Fame has better credentials than Barry Bonds, but thus far the writers have denied him baseball's ultimate honor.

YEAR	TM	G	AB	R	H	HR	RBI	SB	BB	SO	AVG
1986–92	PIT (7 yrs)	1010	3584	672	984	176	556	251	611	590	.275
1993–2007	SFG (15 yrs)	1976	6263	1555	1951	586	1440	263	1947	949	.312
Total (22 yrs)		2986	9847	2227	2935	762	1996	514	2558	1539	.298

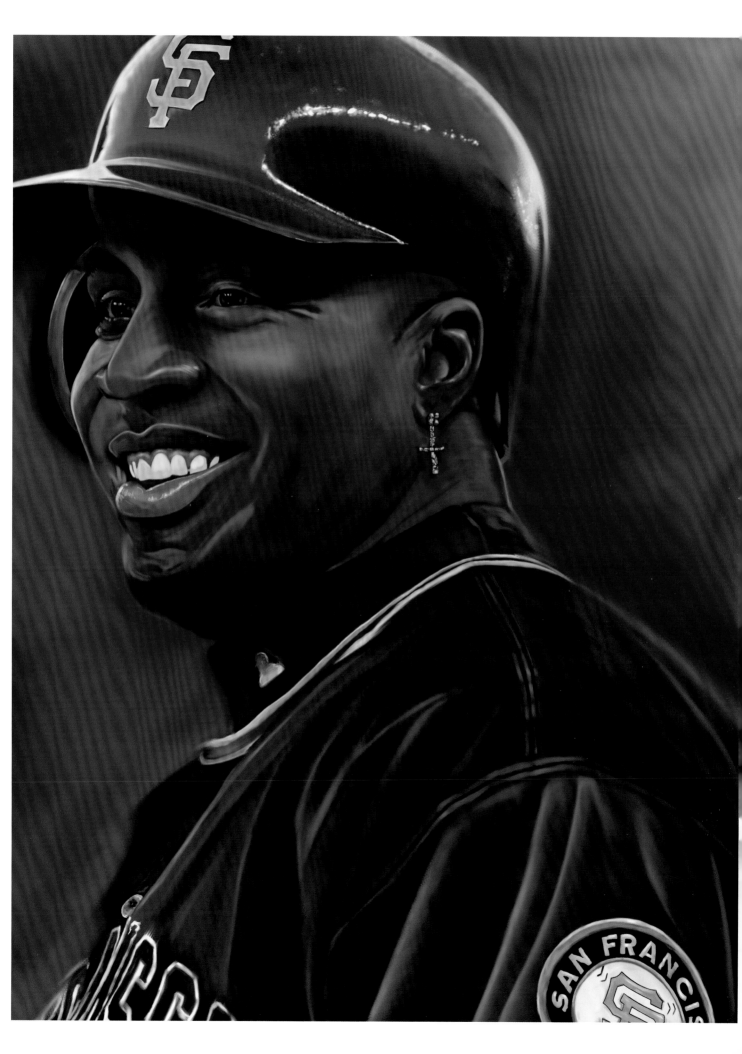

Jeff Kent

When first-year general manager Brian Sabean traded the extremely popular All-Star third baseman Matt Williams to the Cleveland Indians in November 1996 for a mediocre second baseman with a reputation for a bad attitude, San Francisco Giants fans were outraged. "I am not an idiot," said Sabean, a now-recognized front-office genius whose long string of brilliant moves began with the acquisition of Kent, who immediately went on one of the most impressive offensive tears for a player at his position in baseball history.

At age 29, just as players are slowing down, Kent put it all together in his first season (1997) with the Giants. Benefiting from manager Dusty Baker's confidence in him and his place in the lineup, batting cleanup behind Barry Bonds, Kent blasted 29 homers and drove in 121 runs. He was just getting started. He recorded five more consecutive 100+ RBI seasons for the Giants (1998–2002) and then added another in 2004 for the Astros and one more in 2005 for the Dodgers, to give him an unprecedented run of eight 100+ RBI seasons in nine years. During his six-year career with the Giants, Kent helped lead San Francisco to two West Division crowns and a Wild Card playoff berth in 2002. Jeff batted over .300 twice, hit 30 or more home runs three times, set the Giants' season record for doubles (49), and earned three of his four Silver Slugger Awards. He won the NL MVP Award in 2000 and achieved three other Top Ten MVP Award finishes. It was an amazing transformation of a career that had appeared to be going nowhere fast.

Born March 7, 1968, in Bellflower, California, to a state highway motorcycle cop, the young Jeffrey Franklin Kent was always a bit of a loner who liked the individual sports of surfing and motocross as much as baseball. After being kicked off his high school team for what his coach termed "senioritis," Kent played at the University

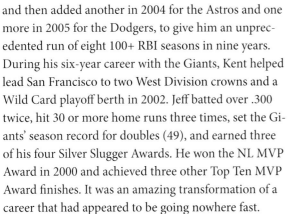

of California, Berkeley, as a walk-on and became the star of the team. He signed with Toronto in 1989 as a 20th-round draft pick and broke into the big leagues three years later. In 1992 he hit .240 in 65 games for the Blue Jays, who traded him to the New York Mets, for whom he finished his rookie season, batting .239 in 37 games.

The Mets teams that Kent played for the next three-and-a-half seasons were terrible, and such ineptitude obscured the progress he was making as a hitter. Kent was not popular with his teammates, and he was also saddled with the label of being a poor defensive player, with limited range and bad hands, making it easy for the Mets to ship him to Cleveland, where he played out the '96 season.

Kent did not win any Gold Gloves with the Giants, but he was capable of making great plays on occasion, and teammates respected his courage, especially in the way he hung tough while making the double play.

Kent's final year (2002) in San Francisco, when the Giants narrowly lost the World Series to the Anaheim Angels, may have been his best, but his .313 average, 37 homers, and 108 RBI were overshadowed by two unfortunate incidents that led to his departure from the team: a broken hand he suffered when he crashed his motorcycle in spring training and an embarrassing midseason shoving match in the dugout with Barry Bonds.

During the final six years of his career, Kent continued to be a productive hitter for both Houston and Los Angeles. On October 2, 2004, he hit his 288th home run to become the all-time home-run leader among second basemen, while in 2005 he led the Dodgers in practically every meaningful batting category. Despite Kent's gaudy offensive statistics, his aloofness and defensive deficiencies make his election to the Baseball Hall of Fame problematic. Not in doubt is the greatness of the six years he spent in the San Francisco Giants uniform.

YEAR	TM	G	AB	R	H	HR	RBI	SB	BB	SO	AVG
1992	TOR (1 yr)	65	192	36	46	8	35	2	20	47	.240
1992–96	NYM (5 yrs)	498	1831	244	510	67	267	12	110	346	.279
1996	CLE (1 yr)	39	102	16	27	3	16	2	10	22	.265
1997–2002	SFG (6 yrs)	900	3434	570	1021	175	689	57	364	659	.297
2003–04	HOU (2 yrs)	275	1045	173	306	49	200	13	88	181	.293
2005–08	LAD (4 yrs)	521	1894	281	551	75	311	8	209	267	.291
Total (17 yrs)		2298	8498	1320	2461	377	1518	94	801	1522	.290

Matt Cain

In the 130-year history of the franchise, no Giants pitcher had ever done it. Not old-timers such as Welch, Keefe, or Rusie. Not even Mathewson, Maglie, or Marichal. Nobody in a Giants uniform had ever pitched a perfect game—until June 13, 2012, when big Matt Cain retired 27 straight batters in a 10–0 win over the Houston Astros at AT&T Park. In honor of the rare achievement, Mayor Ed Lee proclaimed that in San Francisco every future June 13 would be "Matt Cain Day." And, in an even more fitting tribute to a warrior of Cain's caliber, the Mizuno Company, which makes the glove Matt uses, presented him with a Japanese samurai sword.

Matt Cain had been a candidate for the spectacular for some time. In his previous five full seasons with San Francisco, the 6'3", 230-pound right-hander had flirted several times with no-hitters. In fact, on April 13, exactly two months before the perfect game, he had spun the third one-hitter of his career, in the Giants' home opener against Pittsburgh. That match foreshadowed the perfect game, as the sixth-inning single by Pirates pitcher James McDonald resulted in the only base runner Cain allowed in the game.

Sterling catches by Melky Cabrera and Gregor Blanco helped preserve Cain's perfecto, but no one begrudged him the assistance or thought it cheapened the accomplishment, especially given that Cain has been arguably the most hard-luck great pitcher in team history.

A native of Dothan, Alabama, Cain was the Giants' 2002 first-round draft pick out of Germantown, Tennessee's Houston High School, where as a senior he earned state Gatorade Player of the Year honors. Twice *USA Today*'s Organizational Player of the Year, Cain breezed through the Giants' farm system and made his major league debut on August 29, 2005, as the youngest player in San Francisco Giant history. On September 9 he 2-hit the Cubs, becoming the youngest San Francisco Giant to pitch a complete game. His 2.33 ERA and the .151 batting average he held hitters to in 46 IP indicated his talent.

The next year he led NL rookies in wins (13) and strikeouts (179) and became the youngest San Francisco Giant to throw a CG one-hitter. Cain posted losing records in 2007 (7–16) and 2008 (8–14), but those ledgers were mainly the result of weak offensive support. In 2007, for example, the Giants scored two or fewer runs in 21 of Cain's 32 starts, and the bullpen blew five of his leads, yet Matt was the seventh-toughest pitcher in the league to get a hit against (batters hit .235 against him), he turned in the sixth-most (22) quality starts, and his ERA of 3.65 was 10th best.

Despite middling win-loss records, Cain became one of the mainstays in the Giants' rotation and put together an impressive eight-year streak (2006–13), during which he started 30 or more games and compiled 150 or more strikeouts each season. He also finished first twice and eighth once in Quality Starts and was among the 10 most difficult pitchers to hit five more times.

In 2010 Cain was a key contributor to the Giants' run toward the first World Championship in San Francisco history, pitching 21.1 innings over three postseason starts without surrendering an earned run. It was the sixth-longest streak in baseball history. "Big Daddy," as Cain's high school coach called him, was named to the NL All-Star team three times, and he started and won the 2012 contest by pitching two scoreless innings, allowing only one hit. Matt's best year to date came in the "perfect-game year" of 2012, when he reached personal bests in all three Triple Crown categories (16–5/2.88/193). Injuries limited Cain's effectiveness in 2013 and '14, and the need for elbow surgery ended his 2014 season on July 9. Matt returned to action halfway through the 2015 season. While no one could say whether or not his comeback would be completely successful, he will always be fondly remembered as the Giants' "Mr. Perfect."

YEAR	TM	W	L	ERA	GS	CG	SHO	IP	H	R	BB	SO
2005–14	SFG (10 yrs)	95	95	3.39	280	15	6	1811.1	1518	728	611	1506

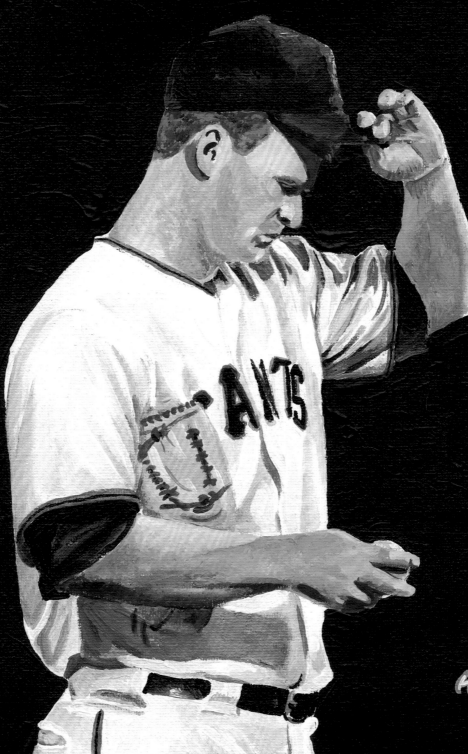

Tim Lincecum

With his long hair and slender build, he looked more like a surfer, a skateboarder, or a bagger at the local grocery than a major league baseball player. It was a radically different story, though, when Timothy Leroy Lincecum started pitching for the San Francisco Giants in 2007. The physically unimposing, undersized kid showed off an ether-splitting fastball and knee-buckling curve that overwhelmed and handcuffed National League hitters, confounded conventional baseball wisdom, and stamped him as the leader of what was one of the best pitching staffs in all of baseball for several years.

Born June 15, 1984, in Bellevue, Washington, Tim Lincecum sneaked up on nobody but newspaper headline writers. He was a pitching prodigy from the time he was four years old, when his father, Chris, a Boeing employee, began teaching him the mechanics that would result in Tim's unorthodox windup and explosive delivery. An exceptional all-around athlete, Lincecum was named Gatorade's Washington Baseball Player of the Year when he led Liberty High School to the 3A State Championship in 2003. The next year, at the University of Washington, he became the first player to be named the Pac-10 Freshman and Player of the Year. He was named an All-American in 2006 and became the Pac-10 all-time strikeout champion.

Lincecum was drafted in the low rounds by the Cubs and Indians, but neither organization really believed the little guy had the stature or stamina to last. Tim signed with the Giants when they made him their number 1 pick (and 10th pick overall) of the 2006 draft, and he proceeded to make a mockery of pro baseball's prejudice against short pitchers. Minor league hitters were helpless against him, and after he went 6–0 in 13 bush league games with 104 strikeouts in 62.1 IP, he got the call to San Francisco.

A 7–5 record and 4.00 ERA in 2007 did not seem impressive, but 150 strikeouts and only 122 hits allowed in 146.1 IP were eye-popping stats, indicating that the Giants had discovered a rare gem of a pitcher. In 2008, in his first full season with the Giants, Lincecum burst into stardom. He became the first Giants pitcher since Mike McCormick to win the Cy Young Award, fashioning an 18–5 record with a 2.62 ERA and a league-leading 265 strikeouts (in 227 innings). Midway through the season, he was introduced to the nation by a *Sports Illustrated* cover story that dissected his mechanics and promulgated a nickname, "The Freak." As an encore, Lincecum won the 2009 NL Cy Young, becoming the first Giants pitcher to win the award twice. He lowered his ERA to 2.48 and led the league in strikeouts again, with 261. He also surrendered only 168 hits in 225.1 innings, continuing a pattern of fewer hits allowed than IP that he has maintained every year of his career.

In 2010 Lincecum went 16–10 and led the NL in strikeouts for the third year in a row; more importantly, though, "The Franchise" led the Giants to the pennant and San Francisco's first-ever World Championship. He was given the Babe Ruth Award as the MVP of the postseason for winning the first game of the NLDS, the NLCS, and the World Series, as well as the Series-clinching Game 5.

Despite a losing record in 2011, Tim had the fourth-best ERA in the league (2.74), and he made the NL All-Star team for the fourth year in a row. He slumped in 2012 but helped the Giants win another World Championship that October by pitching effectively out of the bullpen. He struggled in 2013 and 2014, yet flashed his former brilliance in spinning no-hitters both seasons against the Padres. The owner of the most 10+ strikeout games (31) in Giants history and currently #5 in strikeouts on the franchise's all-time list, Lincecum remains immensely popular with San Francisco fans, who hope to witness the return of the unhittable "Freak."

YEAR	TM	W	L	ERA	GS	CG	SHO	IP	H	R	BB	SO
2007–14	SFG (8 yrs)	101	79	3.59	246	10	7	1567.1	1363	668	608	1644

Pablo Sandoval

During the 2010 World Series, the Giants' slumping, bowling ball–shaped third baseman from Venezuela barely got off the bench. When he got his chance two years later, he made the most of it. In his first three times at bat in Game 1 against Detroit, he hit the ball over the fence (twice off Tigers' ace Justin Verlander), joing Babe Ruth, Reggie Jackson, and Albert Pujols as the only players in history to homer three times in one World Series game. The Giants beat the stunned Tigers 8–3, and the 2012 World Series was essentially over. The legend of Pablo Emilio Sandoval, however, was just beginning.

Born August 11, 1986, in Puerto Cabello, Venezuela, Sandoval was 16 years old when he signed with the Giants in 2003, and he spent his first pro season playing in the Dominican Summer League, batting .354. He was called up to San Francisco in mid-August 2008 after having batted .350 combined for Class A San Jose and AA Connecticut, for which he was named San Francisco Minor League Player of the Year. Sandoval batted .345 in 41 games, astonishing everyone. The 5'11" Sandoval weighed more than 240 pounds, yet he was amazingly agile, athletic enough to score a run in a September game by leaping over the opposing catcher. An aggressive free swinger, he quickly proved himself the best bad-ball hitter in the game, a threat to hit safely any pitch he could reach. He exuded happiness and humility, and after pitcher Barry Zito nicknamed him "Kung Fu Panda" (after the animated movie character) for his "rotund build, lovable nature, and ability to perform remarkable feats," Giants fans adopted him en masse as the team's most popular player.

Having played mostly at first base in the minors, Sandoval became the regular third baseman in 2009 and put together the best year of his career. He hit 44 doubles and 25 home runs and finished second in the NL with a .330 batting average, the fourth-highest average since 1958 for a player in his first full season in the majors.

Sandoval slumped badly in 2010, his weight ballooning to almost 280 pounds. An exercise and nutritional regime called "Operation Panda" helped him slim down, and he rebounded to hit .315 in 2011, despite playing in only 117 games due to a broken hamate bone in his right hand. That year, Pablo enjoyed a 22-game hitting streak and rapped an RBI double in his first All-Star Game appearance. Injuries, including a fracture of his left hamate bone, limited Sandoval to 108 games in 2012, but he set a franchise record with a season-opening 20-game hitting streak, hit the first bases-loaded triple in All-Star Game history, and then put on a spectacular show in the World Series. Pablo batted .500 in the four-game sweep of Detroit and .364 with six homers and 13 RBI over the entire postseason, easily earning himself the MVP awards of both the Series and the postseason.

If the 2012 Fall Classic was Sandoval's coming-out party before a national audience, then 2014 witnessed his coronation as the greatest postseason hitter in Giants history. The Panda batted .400 in the LCS against the Cardinals and .429 in the World Series against the formidable Royals. He ran his streak of getting on base at least once per game during the postseason to 25 games, he had four multihit games in the Series, went 3–3 in Game 7, and set a record for total hits (26) in a postseason. Asked after the Giants' defeat of Kansas City how he was able to excel like this on baseball's grandest stage, he said, "I dunno. I love being under pressure."

Sandoval became a free agent after he caught the foul pop-up that ended the 2014 World Series, and his subsequent signing with the Boston Red Sox disappointed Giants fans everywhere.

YEAR	TM	G	AB	R	H	HR	RBI	SB	BB	SO	AVG
2008–14	SFG (7 yrs)	869	3215	398	946	106	462	11	259	464	.294

Buster Posey

Harry Danning, Gus Mancuso, Wes Westrum, Tom Haller, Bob Brenly: a string of stalwart Giants catchers since the dead ball era. But none the equal of Gerald Dempsey "Buster" Posey III, a legend in the making, who has been the irreplaceable anchor of three Giants World Championship teams in five years.

Posey burst onto the major league baseball scene in 2010 when he won the National League Rookie of the Year Award and led the San Francisco Giants to their first World Championship ever, after the World Series failures of 1962, 1989, and 2002. With his boyish good looks, humble demeanor, and endearing nickname, Buster won Giants fans over in a huge way, yet the party almost ended right after it got started.

On May 25, 2011, in an extra-inning game at AT&T Park, Posey was run over at home plate by the Florida Marlins' Scott Cousins and suffered a serious injury: a broken left fibula and three torn ankle ligaments. Posey, who had come into the game riding a 13-game hitting streak that had boosted his average to .284, was out for the season; and the Giants, in first place at the time of the collision, limped home in second place, 12 games behind the division-winning Arizona Diamondbacks.

Posey's importance not only to the Giants but the game in general was so obvious that major league baseball instituted a rule change to protect catchers facing similar situations in the future. In 2012 Buster bounced back with a vengeance, proving that despite his genial facade he commands all the toughness demanded of his position.

The 6'1", 220-pound Posey (born March 27, 1987) wasn't always a catcher. He pitched and played shortstop at Lee County (Georgia) High School, where he excelled in four sports, and switched to catching as a sophomore at Florida State University. Extremely popular with Seminole fans, Posey won the Johnny Bench and Golden Spikes Awards as a junior and signed with San Francisco after the Giants made him the fifth overall pick of the 2008 draft. Buster got a cup of coffee with the Giants in 2009, and after playing a total of 169 minor league games, he was called up for good in May 2010. Playing mostly first base in the beginning, Posey became the regular catcher by the end of June.

In 2010 Posey became the first rookie to bat cleanup for his team in the World Series, and in 2012 he put his personal stamp on that important slot in the Giants' batting order. The 25-year-old won the National League batting title with an average of .336, a career high, and also set career marks in home runs (24) and RBI (103). He made the NL All-Star team that year (and again in 2013) and led the Giants to a second pennant and second World Championship. He hit three home runs in the postseason, and his game-winning grand slam in Game 5 of the Divisional Series in Cincinnati capped the Giants' historic comeback victory: winning three straight on the road after being behind 2–0. Afterward, the honors poured in. He was voted MVP of the National League, earned a Silver Slugger Award as the best-hitting catcher in the league, and took home multiple Comeback Player of the Year Awards.

Posey's number slid a little in 2013, to .294/15/72, but he roared back in 2014 to win the Giants' batting Triple Crown for the second time. He hit 22 homers, knocked in 89 runs, and batted .311—the third time in four complete seasons he has hit over .300. He won a second Silver Slugger Award and finished sixth in the MVP voting.

After the Giants won it all for the third time in five years with Buster behind the plate, pundits everywhere began to realize what a leader, expert receiver, and savvy pitch-caller he is. Manager Bruce Bochy perfectly summed up his immense value, saying: "We couldn't have done it without Buster. He's been the one constant for us, our driving force. What a great player—and teammate."

YEAR	TM	G	AB	R	H	HR	RBI	SB	BB	SO	AVG
2009–14	SFG (6 yrs)	603	2182	287	673	83	352	6	224	324	.308

Madison Bumgarner

Everything is magnified in the postseason, baseball's crucible. It's in October that baseball becomes more war than sport. It's then that diamond dreams get crushed, and dynasties are born. Excel in the postseason, and you become a star; dominate, and you become a legend—like Madison Kyle Bumgarner, the lionhearted left-hander whose near-invincible pitching carried the San Francisco Giants to the 2014 World Championship.

Bumgarner's historic 2014 postseason performance began with a complete-game four-hit shutout of the Pirates in Pittsburgh in the win-or-go-home NL Wild Card Game. He was named MVP of the NLCS for holding the Cardinals to nine hits in 15.2 innings, and then came the bulldog performance that earned him the MVP Award of the World Series.

In Game 1, he held the Kansas City Royals to one run in seven innings, handing them their first postseason defeat. The run he allowed ended a streak of 32⅔ consecutive scoreless postseason IP on the road and halted another streak of 21 straight scoreless IP to begin a World Series career, the second longest in history (behind Christy Mathewson's streak of 28). Bumgarner pitched another CG four-hit shutout in the crucial Game 5; and then, on two days' rest, he completely shut down the Royals in Game 7, pitching the final five innings in scoreless relief to earn the longest save in World Series history.

When the smoke cleared, Madison had pitched a record 52⅔ postseason innings while posting an ERA of 1.03. Over three World Series he had a 4–0 record and had given up exactly one run in 36 innings for an ERA of 0.25. Even without focusing on the host of records he'd set, Bumgarner had clearly proven himself one of the greatest big-game, "money" pitchers of all time. And he was only 25 years old.

"Madbum," as his teammates call him, had always been a prime-time performer. Ecstatic he was still available,

the Giants took Bumgarner with their first pick in the 2007 draft after the big (6'5", 235 pounds) country boy had led his South Caldwell High team to the 4A North Carolina State Championship. At first, the Giants tinkered with the kid's unorthodox twisting windup and cross-fire delivery, but when he struggled in his first three outings for Single A Augusta, they told him to pitch as he always had. Once Madison got untracked, the minors barely challenged him. In three seasons he went 15–3, 12–2, and 7–1 with a composite ERA of 2.00 as he leapt up the ladder. He made his major league debut September 9, 2009, becoming the second-youngest San Francisco Giant pitcher to start a game. After being called up for good in July 2010, precociousness and intensity became his trademarks.

His 1.13 ERA in five September starts helped the Giants win the 2010 pennant, and in the NLDS against Atlanta he became the youngest pitcher to start and win a postseason game. That year he also became the fourth-youngest pitcher to start and win a World Series game and the second-youngest to throw at least eight scoreless innings in a Series game. He was named to *Baseball America*'s All-Rookie Team.

Because of poor run support, Bumgarner's record in 2011 was deceptive. He may have finished 13–13, but in games in which the Giants scored three or more runs, he went 12–1. He won 16 games and twirled seven more scoreless World Series innings in 2012 and then made the NL All-Star team in 2013, turning in the league's fifth-best ERA (2.77).

In 2014 Bumgarner became the unquestioned ace of the Giants' staff. He made his first Opening Day start and copped the team's pitching Triple Crown with an 18–10 record, an ERA of 2.98, and 219 strikeouts. A dangerous hitter who takes fearsome cuts, he also stroked a pair of grand slams. It was all a warm-up for his legendary postseason.

YEAR	TM	W	L	ERA	GS	CG	SHO	IP	H	R	BB	SO
2009–14	SFG (6 yrs)	67	49	3.06	148	6	3	952.2	852	360	229	896